# دليل الصلاة
# A Guide To Salât (Prayer)

*by*

**Muhammad Abdul Karim Saqib**
Birmingham, U.K.

**DARUSSALAM**
GLOBAL LEADER IN ISLAMIC BOOKS
Riyadh • Jeddah • Al-Khobar • Sharjah
Lahore • London • Houston • New York

بسم الله الرحمن الرحيم

*"In the Name of Allâh*
*The Most Beneficent, the Most Merciful"*

2nd Edition: December 2013



King Fahd National Library Catalog-in-Publication Data

**Saqib, Mohammad Abdul Karim**

A guide to Salat (Prayer) –Riyadh.

64p, 14x21 cm.

**ISBN: 9960-717-17-8**

1- Prayer II-Title

252.3dc 2363/17

**Legal Deposit no. 2363/17**

**ISBN: 9960-717-17-8**

# Contents

## *Chapter 4*



## *Chapter 5*

# Foreword

There are many books dealing with the subject of *Ṣalât* in both Arabic and Urdu. Many of these books are well written and provide an informative and comprehensive view of how *Ṣalât* should be performed according to the teachings of Prophet Muḥammad (ﷺ). Unfortunately, there are very few books in English which deal with the subject in the same informative and comprehensive way. The books, which do exist, have three main disadvantages:

***Firstly,*** literature concerning *Ṣalât* available in English is either so brief that it does not cover essential points in nearly enough detail, or it is so bulky and detailed that it becomes difficult to use it for quick reference, and essential points may get lost in the unnecessary detail.

***Secondly,*** the text of the *Ṣalât* lacks the quality of direct research from the *Sunnah* of the Prophet Muḥammad (ﷺ). There are also books which contain material without any reference to the original sources.

***Thirdly,*** the majority of books have been written according to the views held by certain schools of thought and for this reason some people hesitate to follow them.

Because of these weaknesses in existing literature in English, we felt that the need existed to produce a medium sized book on *Ṣalât* which would approach the subject according to the teachings of the Prophet Muḥammad (ﷺ). The Prophet, himself, said:

«صَلُّوا كَمَا رَأَيْتُمُونِي أُصَلِّي»

*"Pray as you have seen me praying."*

Such a book needs to contain all the essential details of *Ṣalât* without being too bulky or complicated so that the reader can use it as a point of reference on a journey or at home.

It was also felt that a comprehensive book on *Ṣalât* in English would be useful for converts to Islam and for such Muslims who do not fully understand Arabic and Urdu languages. Keeping in mind the needs of our brothers and sisters, every effort has been made to produce this book in simple and easy language.

During our research, we sometimes found that differences occurred between established practices in various prayer books. In these circumstances we referred to authentic *Aḥâdith* of the Prophet Muḥammad (ﷺ), so that the points could be clarified as much as possible. This was, because, for a true Muslim there is no greater proof for settling arguments than authentic *Aḥâdith* and practices of Prophet Muḥammad (ﷺ).

We hope that Allâh will accept this humble attempt because without His Support and Help we would never have been able to do this work.

Finally, we ask all our Muslim brothers and sisters to study the text and to strive to offer *Ṣalât* (prayer) according to it. If anyone finds anything unacceptable or to be against the *Sunnah* of the Prophet (ﷺ) we would be grateful if they would inform us.

***Muḥammad Abdul Karim Saqib***

# Notes about the Transliteration

The following system has been adopted to represent corresponding sounds of the Arabic alphabet:

| Arabic Letter | English Equivalent | Example (Arabic) | Example (English) |
|---|---|---|---|
| ا | a | Allâh | apple |
| ب | b | Bismillâh | bat |
| ت | t | Tirmidhi | Talmud |
| ث | th | Uthmân | through |
| ج | j | Jâbir | jug |
| ح | ḥ | Raḥeem | hate |
| خ | kh | Khalifah | (no English equivalent) |
| د | d | Darmi | the |
| ذ | dh | Adhân | resemble |
| ر | r | Aṣr | river |
| ز | z | Zahid | zero |
| س | s | Salâm | seen |
| ش | sh | Shuaib | shop |
| ص | ṣ | Ṣalât | sardine |
| ض | ḍ | Wuḍu | (no equivalent) |
| ط | ṭ | Ṭahir | (no equivalent) |
| ظ | ẓ | Ẓuhr | razor |

| | | | |
|---|---|---|---|
| ع | ‘ | Jamâ‘at | (no equivalent) |
| غ | gh | Maghrib | (no equivalent) |
| ف | f | Fajr | fan |
| ق | q | Iqâmat | queen |
| ك | k | Kitâb | keen |
| ل | l | Jibrael | lean |
| م | m | Muḥammad | moon |
| ن | n | Nasâi | noon |
| و | w | Wuḍu | wallet |
| هـ | h | Janâzah | hour |
| ء | ’ | | (no equivalent) |
| (in the middle of the letter) | | | |
| ى | y | | year |

The following system has been adopted to represent some of the complex sounds of the Arabic language:

A macro (-) placed on a transcribed Arabic vowel indicates lengthening of the sound of the letter.

| Arabic | English Equivalent | Example (Arabic) | Example (English) |
|---|---|---|---|
| آ | â | Allâh | apple |
| اِي | ee | Raheem | seen |
| اِ | i | Istinja | sit |
| ء | i or ee | | seen |
| هِـ | hî | | he |
| اُ | u | | boot |

| | | | |
|---|---|---|---|
| أُوْ | û | Dawûd | true |
| اَوْ | aw | | sew |
| اَوّ | aww | awwal | Shovel |
| اَيْ | ay | | bay |
| اَيّ | ayy | | age |
| اِيّ | iyy | | |

***Note:*** Sometimes an Arabic letter changes sound according to its position in the word; for example; whether it is at the beginning, in the middle or at the end. In such circumstances the Arabic letter has been represented by more than one English equivalent.

# Abbreviations

The following abbreviations have been used in this book:-

| | |
|---|---|
| (ﷺ) | **ṢAL-LAL LÂHU 'ALAYHI WA SAL-LAM**<br>(Peace And Blessing Of Allâh Be Upon Him) |
| (رضي الله عنه) | **RAḌI ALLÂHU 'ANHU**<br>(May Allâh Be Pleased With Him) |
| (رضي الله عنها) | **RAḌI ALLÂHU 'ANHA**<br>(May Allâh Be Pleased With Her) |
| (رضي الله عنهما) | **RAḌI ALLÂHU 'ANHUMA**<br>(May Allâh Be Pleased With Them) |
| (رضي الله عنهم) | **RAḌI ALLÂHU 'ANHUM**<br>(May Allâh Be Pleased With Them) |
| (رحمه الله) | **RAHIMAHULLAH**<br>(May Allâh's Mercy Be Upon Him) |
| (رحمهم الله) | **RAHIMAHUMLLAH**<br>(May Allâh's Mercy Be Upon Them). |

Chapter 1

# *Wuḍu* (Ablution)

## *Before Doing Wuḍu (Ablution)*

If someone needs to go to the toilet, he should use the toilet and do *Istinja* before doing *Wuḍu.*

## *Siwak (Tooth-Stick)*

It is good practice to clean the teeth with a tooth-stick, or a tooth-brush before performing *Wuḍu.* In this way you can avoid many diseases which are caused by unclean teeth.

As mentioned in the *Ḥadith*: 'Âisha (ﷺ) reported Allâh's Messenger as saying:

> *"The use of a tooth-stick is a means of purifying the mouth and is pleasing to the Lord as well."* (Aḥmad, Dârmi and Nasâi)

Prophet Muḥammad (ﷺ) also said:

> *"If I wouldn't have felt that it is difficult for my people I would have ordered them to use a tooth-stick with every Ṣalât (prayer), that is, before doing each Wuḍu."*

So, Muslims should always try to fulfil this wish of our Prophet (ﷺ).

## *Making Intention (Niyat) for Wuḍu*

Before starting the actions of *Wuḍu* it is necessary to make *Niyat.* Make *Niyat* that the act of performing *Wuḍu* is for the purpose of purity only. *Niyat* should be made in the heart because it is an action of the heart and not of the tongue.

*Niyat* by words is not approved by Prophet Muḥammad (ﷺ).

Then start the *Wuḍu* by saying:

*"Bismillâh hir-Raḥmanir-Raḥeem."*

"In the Name of Allâh, the Most Gracious, the Most Merciful."

**Actions for performing *Wuḍu* (Ablution):**

1. Wash the hands up to the wrist making sure that no part of the hands is left dry.
2. Rinse the mouth taking up water with the right hand.
3. Clean the nose: sniff water up from the right palm and then eject water with the left hand.
4. Wash the face, from ear to ear, and forehead to chin making sure that no part of the face is left dry.
5. Then wash the forearms (right forearm first) up to the elbows making sure that no part of them is left dry.
6. Rub the head as follows: Wet your fingers and then wipe the head with your fingers, starting from the forehead, taking them to the nape of the neck, then bring them back to the forehead.
7. Clean the ears by inserting the tips of the index fingers wetted with water into the ears, twist them around the folds of the ears then pass the thumb behind the ears from the bottom, upwards.
8. Wash the feet (right foot first) up to the ankles making sure that no parts of the feet are left dry, especially between the toes.

**Special facilities in *Wuḍu* (Ablution):**

Rubbing the socks with wet hands instead of washing the feet is allowed provided that the socks have been put on after performing an ablution, including washing the feet. This is allowed for 24 hours from the time of ablution, and for 3 days if the person is on a journey. After this time the feet must be washed. Similarly if there is a wound in any parts of the body which has to be washed in ablution, and if washing that particular part is likely to cause harm, it is permissible to wipe the dressing of the wound with a wet hand.

***Ḥadith*:**

Mughira bin Shu'bah said:

> *"Prophet (ﷺ) performed ablution and wiped over his socks and his sandals."* (Aḥmad, Tirmidhi, Abu Dâwûd and Ibn Mâjah)

Each detail of ablution has been performed by Prophet Muḥammad (ﷺ) once, twice or three times (except rubbing of head and cleaning of ears, i.e. actions 6 and 7 should only be done once). Since all the above methods meet Prophet's (ﷺ) approval; we can perform ablution by doing the actions once, twice or three times; provided that no part has been left dry.

'Amr bin Shu'aib, quoting his father on the authority of his grandfather narrated that Prophet Muḥammad (ﷺ) said:

> *"If anyone performs actions of ablution more than 3 times, he has done wrong, transgressed, and done wickedly."* (Nasâi and Ibn Mâjah)

## Du'â at the end of Wuḍu (Ablution)

«أَشْهَدُ أَنْ لَا إِلَهَ إِلَّا اللهُ وَحْدَهُ لَاشَرِيْكَ لَهُ وَأَشْهَدُ أَنَّ مُحَمَّدًا عَبْدُهُ وَرَسُوْلُهُ»

(مسلم)

*"Ash hadu an lâ ilâha illal lâhu waḥ dahu lâ shareeka lahu wa ash hadu an-na Muḥammadan 'abduhu wa Rasûluhu."*

"I testify that there is no deity except Allâh Alone. And I testify that Muḥammad (ﷺ) is His servant and Messenger." (Muslim)

«اللَّهُمَّ اجْعَلْنِي مِنَ التَّوَّابِينَ وَاجْعَلْنِي مِنَ الْمُتَطَهِّرِينَ» (ترمذي)

*"Allâhum maj 'alnee minat taw-wâbeena waj 'alnee minal muta ṭah-hireen."*

"O Allâh make me among those who are penitent and make me among those who are purified." (Tirmidhi)

## *Tayammum*

In circumstances when water cannot be found, or just enough is available for drinking, or it is injurious to health: in such situations *Tayammum* (dry ablution) can be performed.

The procedure below is given according to Qur'ân and *Ḥadith*.

*"...And if you don't find any water, then take clean earth (or sand) and rub it on your face, and hands. Allâh does not wish to put you in a difficulty, but He wants to make you clean, and to complete His Favour unto you, so you should be grateful to Him."* (*Surah* 5, *Verse*:6)

(The permission to use sand for this purpose is allowed in the Qur'ân).

**Procedure:**

1. Make *Niyat* in the heart.
2. Begin with the Name of Allâh.
3. Strike palms of both hands on clean sand, dust or anything containing these, e.g. wall or stone etc. then blow into the palms. Pass the palms of both hands over the face once and then rub your right hand with the left palm and left hand with the right palm. (Bukhâri and Muslim)
4. Finish with the same *Du'â* as given at the end of ablution.

***Note:*** Other procedures include the forearms and shoulders as well as armpits. These have been transmitted by reputable scholars but the most preferable and authentic is that given above.

Chapter 2

# Time-Place-Dress and Types of *Ṣalât*

## *Time of Ṣalât:*

Each *Ṣalât* must be offered at or during its proper time. No *Ṣalât* can be offered before its time. There are five obligatory *Ṣalât* in a day:

***Fajr Prayer***: The time for the *Fajr* or the morning prayer starts at dawn and ends at sunrise.

***Ẓuhr Prayer***: The time for *Ẓuhr* or the early afternoon prayer starts when the sun begins to decline from its zenith and ends when the size of an objects's shadow is equal to the size of the object.

Jâbir bin 'Abdullâh (ﷺ) narrated: "The angel Jibrael came to Prophet Muḥammad (ﷺ) and said to him, "Stand up and pray *Ẓuhr."* So Allâh's Messenger (ﷺ) prayed *Ẓuhr* when the sun had declined from its zenith. Then the angel Jibrael came again at the time of *'Aṣr* and said, "Stand up and pray *'Aṣr*." Then Prophet Muḥammad (ﷺ) prayed *'Aṣr* when the shadow of everything was equal to itself. Then Jibrael came the next day to Prophet Muḥammad (ﷺ) and said, "Stand up and pray *Ẓuhr*." Then Prophet Muḥammad (ﷺ) prayed *Ẓuhr* when the shadow of everything was equal to itself. Then Jibrael came again at *'Aṣr* time and said, "Stand up and pray *'Aṣr*." Then he prayed *'Aṣr* when the shadow of everything was twice its length...Then Jibrael said, (after praying 10 *Ṣalât* with Prophet Muḥammad (ﷺ) in two consecutive days) that the time of *Ṣalât* (prayer) is in between these two times."

Aḥmad, Nasâi, Tirmidhi and Bukhâri remarked that this is the most authentic *Ḥadith* giving the times of prayer.

We find that many books on *Ṣalât* state the ending time of *Ẓuhr* prayer and the starting time of *'Aṣr* prayer when the shadow of something is twice itself. But this contradicts the above Ḥadith as on the first day Jibrael asked Prophet Muḥammad (ﷺ) to pray *'Aṣr* when the shadow of everything was equal to itself. This means that was the end time of *Ẓuhr* prayer. And we already know that all the *'Ulamâ* of the Muslim *Ummah* agree unanimously that no *Ṣalât* (prayer) can be offered before its time.

***'Aṣr Prayer:*** The time for *'Aṣr* or late afternoon prayer starts when the shadow of something is equal to itself and ends just before sunset.

It is better to offer *'Aṣr* prayer before the sun becomes yellow because even though it is allowed to offer the *Ṣalât* (prayer) at this time the Prophet (ﷺ) disliked Muslims to delay *'Aṣr* prayer up to this time. He remarked that the *Munâfiq* (hypocrite) offered his *Ṣalât* (prayer) at this time.

***Maghrib Prayer:*** The time for the *Maghrib* or the sunset prayer starts just after sunset and ends when twilight has disappeared.

***'Ishâ* Prayer:** The time for *'Ishâ* or night prayer starts from the disappearance of twilight and ends just before midnight.

It is preferable to offer this *Ṣalât* (prayer) before midnight but it can be offered right up to the break of dawn.

***Note:*** In countries due to cloudy weather the sun is not always visible, it is advisable to follow printed calendars giving the accurate time of each *Ṣalât* (prayer).

## Forbidden Times of Prayer:

Uqbah bin 'Âmir said: "There were three times at which Allâh's Messenger (ﷺ) used to forbid us to pray or bury our dead:

i) When the sun began to rise until it was fully up.

ii) When the sun was at its height at midday till it passed the meridian.

iii) When the sun drew near to setting till it had set." (Muslim)

**Forbidden Times for *Nafl* Prayer:**

i) Abu Sa'eeed Al-Khudree (رضي الله عنه) reported Allâh's Messenger (ﷺ) as saying, "No *Ṣalât* (prayer) is to be said after the *Fajr* prayer until the sun rises, or after the *'Aṣr* prayer until the sun sets." (Bukhâri and Muslim)

Only *Nafl* prayer is forbidden at these times but a missed *Farḍ* prayer can be offered. Most of the *'Ulamâ* of the Muslim *Ummah* allowed the offering of missed *Farḍ* prayer after *Fajr* and *'Aṣr* because of the following *Ḥadith*:

Prophet Muḥammad (ﷺ) said, "Who has forgotten the prayer the should pray it whenever he remembers it." (Bukhâri and Muslim)

ii) A *Nafl* prayer cannot be offered once the *Iqâmat* for *Farḍ* prayer has been said. Abu Hurairah narrated that Allâh's Messenger (ﷺ) said, "When the *Iqâmat* has been said, then, there is no *Ṣalât* (prayer) valid (*Nafl* or *Sunnat*) except the *Farḍ* prayer for which the *Iqâmat* was said." (Aḥmad and Muslim)

It is seen in practice that many people continue with the *Sunnat* prayer even though the *Iqâmat* has been said for the *Farḍ* prayer especially in the *Fajr* prayer. They feel that 2 *Rak'at Sunnat* of *Fajr* can only be offered before the *Farḍ*. This practice is against congergation philosophy, discipline of *Jamâ'at,* and a clear violation of *Ḥadith*. They should offer 2 *Rak'at Sunnat* of *Fajr* immediately after the *Farḍ* or after sunrise.

## Place for Ṣalât

A place or a building which is used for the purpose of worship and *Ṣalât* (prayer) is called a *Masjid* (mosque). A *Ḥadith* tells us that "All the earth has been rendered for the Muslims, a mosque (pure and clean)."

This means that wherever a Muslim might be, he can offer his *Ṣalât* (prayer) but the reward of a *Ṣalât* (prayer) offered in a mosque is far greater than that offered in an ordinary place. The following points should be noted when choosing a place for *Ṣalât* (prayer):

a) The place should be clean and pure. *Ṣalât* in a dirty, filthy and impure place such as a rubbish tip, slaughter house, bathing place and a camel pen is forbidden.

b) The place should be free from danger. The danger could be due to someone or something that may disturb the worshipper.

c) A prayer place where the worshipper might hinder the movement of others should be avoided, e.g. busy pavements, public roadways etc.

d) It is forbidden to pray on the roof of *Baitullâh* (Ka'bah).

e) It is forbidden to pray on top of or facing towards a grave.

## *Dress for Ṣalât*

**Men:**

i) The dress for men should be such that it covers from the navel to the knees at least.

ii) The shoulders should not be left uncovered.

iii) *Ṣalât* can be prayed in one garment if it covers the body from the navel to the knees as well as the shoulders.

*"None of you must pray in a single garment of which no part comes over the shoulder."* (Bukhâri and Muslim)

If, however, the garment is not long enough to cover the shoulders then parts of the body between the navel and the knees should at least be covered.

**Women:**

The dress of the woman should be such that it covers her whole body from head to foot leaving only the face and the hands uncovered. A *Ṣalât* (prayer) offered in transparent clothing is not valid. Also tight fitting clothing which shows the shape of the body should be avoided.

## *Types of Ṣalât*

### *a) Farḍ or obligatory Ṣalât*

*Farḍ* prayer is an obligatory prayer. Every beliver is ordered by Allâh to offer five obligatory prayers in a day. Failure to observe any one of the five obligatory prayers is a serious and punishable sin.

***b) Nafl prayer***

This is a voluntary prayer which the Prophet (ﷺ) observed before or after *Farḍ* at special and isolated occasions. It also includes those which he encouraged Muslims to pray.

The *Nafl* prayer can be divided into three categories:

i) *Sunnat Mu'akkadah* (compulsory)

That is those which are emphasized by the holy Prophet (ﷺ) and offered regularly by him before or after the *Farḍ* prayer.

ii) *Sunnat Ghair Mu'akkadah* (optional)

That is those offered only occasionally by Prophet Muḥammad (ﷺ).

iii) *Nafl* prayer (extra)

This is an extra prayer. There is a reward for praying it and no sin for leaving it. It can be offered at any isolated instance according to the time and capacity of the believer. Prophet Muḥammad (ﷺ) encouraged the believers to pray *Nafl* to help make up for any minor omissions or other defects in the obligatory prayer.

**Number of Rak'at for the five obligatory Prayers:**

i) *Fajr* prayer. 2 *Rak'at Sunnat Mu'akkadah,* 2 *Rak'at Farḍ.*

ii) *Ẓurh* prayer. 2 or 4 *Rak'at Sunnat Mu'akkadah,* 4 *Rak'at Farḍ,* 2 *Rak'at Sunnat Mu'akkadah* and an unspecified number of *Nafl* as time and capacity allows.

Ibn 'Umar (رضي الله عنه) said: "I prayed alone with Allâh's Messenger (ﷺ) 2 *Rak'at* before and 2 *Rak'at* after the *Ẓuhr* prayer." (Bukhâri and Muslim)

It is a familiar practice to offer 4 *Rak'at Sunnat* before *Ẓuhr* prayer, but this *Ḥadith* proves that 2 *Rak'at Sunnat* after the *Ẓuhr* prayer is also allowed.

iii) *'Aṣr* prayer. 2 or 4 *Rak'at Sunnat Ghair Mu'akkadah,* 4 *Rak'at Farḍ.* 'Ali (رضي الله عنه) said: "Allâh's Messenger (ﷺ) used to pray 4 *Rak'at* before *'Aṣr* prayer separating them with a salutation ... " (Tirmidhi)

Another *Ḥadith* narrated by 'Ali (ﷺ) says, "Allâh's Messenger (ﷺ) used to pray two *Rak'at* before *'Aṣr* prayer." (Abu Dâwûd)

iv) *Maghrib* prayer. 2 *Rak'at Nafl,* 3 *Rak'at Farḍ,* 2 *Rak'at Sunnat Mu'akkadah* and an unspecified number of *Nafl* as time and capacity allows.

'Abdullâh bin Mughaffal reported the Prophet (ﷺ) as saying:

*"Pray before the Maghrib prayer", adding when saying it the third time, "This applies to those who wish to do so."* (Bukhâri and Muslim)

That was because he did not wish people to treat it as a compulsory *Sunnat.*

2 *Rak'at Nafl* after sunset and before the *Maghrib* prayer are allowed for those who wish to do so. For this the above *Ḥadith* is a sure proof. However, some people forbid this and others find it very strange if they see a person offer 2 *Rak'at Nafl* before *Maghrib.*

v) *'Ishâ* prayer. An unspecified number of *Nafl Rak'at* according to the time and capacity, 4 *Rak'at Farḍ,* 2 *Rak'at Sunnat Mu'akkadah,* unspecified number of *Nafl* as time and capacity allows and 3 *Witr.*

Some people insist very emphatically upon the offering of 4 *Rak'at* optional *Sunnat* before the *'Ishâ* prayer but during our entire research we could not find a single proof, any practice or order from Prophet Muḥammad (ﷺ) or his companions to justify this claim. Certainly it is allowed to pray *Nafl* while waiting for *Jamâ'at.*

Some people offer 3 *Rak'at Nafl* after the *Witr* prayer. However, there is an authentic *Ḥadith* which states that the *Witr* prayer should be offered after all the *Nafl,* which a person wishes to pray, have been offered.

Ibn 'Umar (ﷺ) reported that Allâh's Messenger (ﷺ) said:

*"Make Witr as the last prayer of your night prayer."* (Mishkât)

Chapter 3

# Adhân... Iqâmat

As you know, in all Muslim countries *Adhân* is called aloud five times a day and you must have heard it. Have you ever wondered how it started?

## The Story of Adhân

"A long time ago when the Muslims migrated from Makkah to Al-Madinah they used to agree about a fixed time for the congregational prayer. But they found it difficult to remember the time fixed for the *Ṣalât* (prayer) sometimes, especially when they were busy doing their work. One day Prophet Muḥammad (ﷺ) and the Muslims discussed the matter of calling the people for the congregational prayer at the exact time. Some of the believers suggested the use of something like the bell of the Christians, others suggested the use of a horn like that of the Jews, but 'Umar (رضي الله عنه) suggested sending someone to announce the prayer. Then Allâh's Messenger (ﷺ) appointed Bilâl to call the people to prayer. But it seems through the study of *Aḥadith* that the method was not satisfactory. Then Prophet Muḥammad (ﷺ) agreed to use a *Nâqoose* (a conch), something like the bell of Christians but he was not happy to use it because of its similarity with the Christians.

After Prophet Muḥammad (ﷺ) had ordered a bell to be made so that it could be struck to gather the people to *Ṣalât* (prayer); on that same day a companion, 'Abdullâh bin Zaid bin Abd Rabbihi, said, "I was sleeping when I saw a man carrying a *Naqoose* in his hands, and I said, "Servant of Allâh, will you sell this to me?" When he asked what I would do with it? I replied that we would use it to call the people to *Ṣalât* (prayer). He said, "Shall I not guide you to something better than that?" I replied, "Certainly", so he told me to say:

*"Allâhu Akbar, Allâhu Akbar, Allâhu Akbar, Allâhu Akbar; Ash hadu an-lâ ilâha illal lâh, Ash hadu an-lâ ilâha illal lâh;*

*Ash hadu an-na Muḥammadar Rasûlul-lâh, Ash hadu an-na Muḥammadar Rasûlul-lâh; Ḥayya 'alaṣ ṣalâh, Ḥayya 'alaṣ ṣalâh; Ḥayya 'alal falâḥ, Ḥayya 'alal falâḥ; Allâhu Akbar, Allâhu Akbar; lâ ilâha illal lâh."*

After the *Adhân* the stranger kept quiet for a while and then said: "When the congregation is ready, you should say: *Allâhu Akbar, Allâhu Akbar; Ash hadu an-lâ ilâha illal lâh; Ash hadu an-na Muḥammadar Rasûlul-lâh; Ḥayya 'alaṣ ṣalâh; Ḥayya 'alal falâḥ; Qad qâma tiṣ ṣalâh, qad qâma tiṣ ṣalâh; Allâhu Akbar, Allâhu Akbar; lâ ilâha illal lâh.*

When I told Allâh's Messenger (ﷺ) in the morning what I had seen, he said, "It is a ture vision, *Inshâ-Allâh,* so get up along with Bilâl, and when you have taught him what you have seen, let him use it in making the call to *Ṣalât* (prayer), for he has stronger voice than you have."

So I got up along with Bilâl and began to teach it to him, and he used it in making the call to *Ṣalât* (prayer).

'Umar bin Al-Khaṭṭâb heard this when he was in his house, and he came out trailing his cloak and said, "Allâh's Messenger (ﷺ), by Him, Who has sent you with the truth, I have seen the same kind of thing as has been revealed." To this Allâh's Messenger (ﷺ) replied, "Praise be to Allâh!" (Dârmi, Aḥmad, Ibn Mâjah, Ibn Khuzaimah and Tirmidhi)

So from that day on to the present day *Adhân* is said to gather people for the congregational prayer.

## The Mu'adhin

A person who calls people for the congregational prayer is called a *Mu'adhin*. Before saying the *Adhân,* he should stand facing *Ka'bah* in Makkah. He should raise his hands to his ears putting the tips of forefingers into his ears and call in a loud voice. When he says *Ḥayya 'alaṣ ṣalâh* he should turn his face to the right and when he says *Ḥayya 'alal falâḥ* he should turn his faced to the left.

***Text of the Adhân:***

| | |
|---|---|
| *Allâhu Akbar, Allâhu Akbar,* | اللهُ أَكْبَرُ، اللهُ أَكْبَرُ، |
| Allâh is the Greatest, Allâh is the Greatest. | |
| *Allâhu Akbar, Allâhu Akbar.* | اللهُ أَكْبَرُ اللهُ أَكْبَرُ. |
| Allâh is the Greatest, Allâh is the Greatest. | |
| *Ash hadu an-lâ ilâha illal lâh.* | أَشْهَدُ أَنْ لَا إِلٰهَ إِلَّااللهُ، |
| I bear witness that there is no deity but Allâh. | |
| *Ash hadu an-lâ ilâha illal lâh,* | أَشْهَدُ أَنْ لَا إِلٰهَ إِلَّااللهُ. |
| I bear witness that there is no deity but Allâh. | |
| *Ash hadu an-na Muḥammadar Rasûlul-lâh,* | أَشْهَدُ أَنَّ مُحَمَّدًا رَسُولُ اللهِ، |
| I bear witness that Muḥammad (ﷺ) is Allâh's Messenger. | |
| *Ash hadu an-na Muḥammadar Rasûlul-lâh.* | أَشْهَدُ أَنَّ مُحَمَّدًا رَسُولُ اللهِ. |
| I bear witness that Muḥammad (ﷺ) is Allâh's Messenger. | |
| *Ḥayya 'alaṣ ṣalâh, Ḥayya 'alaṣ ṣalâh.* | حَيَّ عَلَى الصَّلَاةِ، حَيَّ عَلَى الصَّلَاةِ |
| Come to the Prayer, Come to the Prayer. | |
| *Ḥayya 'alal falâḥ, Ḥayya 'alal falâḥ.* | حَيَّ عَلَى الْفَلَاحِ، حَيَّ عَلَى الْفَلَاحِ |
| Come to your good, Come to your good. | |
| *Allâhu Akbar, Allâhu Akbar.* | اللهُ أَكْبَرُ ، اللهُ أَكْبَرُ |
| Allâh is the Greatest, Allâh is the Greatest. | |
| *lâ ilâha illal lâh.* | لَا إِلٰهَ إِلَّا اللهُ. |
| There is no deity but Allâh. | |

**A<u>dh</u>ân for *Fajr*:**

An additional phrase is include in the *A<u>dh</u>ân* for the *Fajr* prayer after the second *Ḥayya 'alal falâḥ*

«الصَّلَاةُ خَيْرٌ مِّنَ النَّوْمِ، الصَّلَاةُ خَيْرٌ مِّنَ النَّوْمِ»

*"Aṣ ṣalâtu <u>kh</u>ayrum minan nawm, Aṣ ṣalâtu <u>kh</u>ayrum minan nawm."*

"Prayer is better than sleep, Prayer is better than sleep."

**Listening to the *A<u>dh</u>ân*:**

1) When the believers hear the *A<u>dh</u>ân* they should listen to it in silence and repeat each phrase of the *A<u>dh</u>ân* in silence immediately after the *Mua'<u>dh</u>in* has finished saying the phrase.
2) When the *Mua'<u>dh</u>in* says: "*Ḥayya 'alaṣ ṣalâh* and *Ḥayya 'alal falâḥ* the listener should say in reply:

«لَا حَولَ وَلَا قُوَّةَ إِلَّا بِاللهِ»

*"La ḥawla wala quwwata illa bil-lâh."*

3) When the *A<u>dh</u>ân* has been completed, the listener and the *Mua'<u>dh</u>in* recite *Darûd* unto Muḥammad (ﷺ) followed by the *Du'â*.

## Darûd after the A<u>dh</u>ân

«اللَّهُمَّ صَلِّ عَلَى مُحَمَّدٍ وَعَلَى آلِ مُحَمَّدٍ ، كَمَا صَلَّيْتَ عَلَى إِبْرَاهِيمَ وَعَلَى آلِ إِبْرَاهِيمَ إِنَّكَ حَمِيدٌ مَّجِيدٌ. اللَّهُمَّ بَارِكْ عَلَى مُحَمَّدٍ وَعَلَى آلِ مُحَمَّدٍ ، كَمَا بَارَكْتَ عَلَى إِبْرَاهِيمَ وَعَلَى آلِ إِبْرَاهِيمَ إِنَّكَ حَمِيدٌ مَّجِيدٌ»

*"Allâhumma ṣali-li 'ala Muḥammadin wa 'ala âli Muḥammadin kamâ ṣal-layta 'ala Ibrâheema wa 'ala âli Ibrâheema innaka Ḥameedun Majeed. Allâhumma bârik 'ala Muḥammadin wa 'ala âli Muḥammadin kamâ bârakta 'ala Ibrâheema wa 'ala âli Ibrâheema innaka Ḥameedun Majeed."*

"Oh Allâh, let your peace come upon Muḥammad (ﷺ) and the family of Muḥammad (ﷺ) as You have sent peace upon Ibrâheem (عليه السلام) and his family. Truly You are Praiseworthy and Glorious. Oh Allâh, bless Muḥammad (ﷺ) and the family of Muḥammad (ﷺ) as You have blessed Ibrâheem (عليه السلام) and his family. Truly You are Praiseworthy and Glorious."

## *Du'â after the Adhân*

«اللَّهُمَّ رَبَّ هَذِهِ الدَّعْوَةِ التَّامَّةِ وَالصَّلَاةِ الْقَ آئِمَةِ آتِ مُحَمَّدًا الْوَسِيْلَةَ وَالْفَضِيْلَةَ وَابْعَثْهُ مَقَامًا مَّحْمُوْدًا الَّذِىْ وَعَدْتَّهُ»

*"Allâhumma rabba hâdhi hid da'wa tit tâm mati waṣ ṣalâ til qâ'imati âti Muḥammada nil waseelata wal faḍeelata wab 'ath-hu maqâmam mahmûda nil ladhi wa'ad tahu."*

"Oh Allâh! Lord of this complete prayer of ours. By the blessing of it, give Muḥammad (ﷺ) his eternal rights of intercession, distinction and highest class (in Paradise). And raise him to the promised rank You have promised him.

Jâbir (رضي الله عنه) reported Allâh's Messenger (ﷺ) as saying:

*"If anyone says when he hears the Adhân, 'O God, Lord of this perfect call and of the prayer which is established for all time, grant Muḥammad (ﷺ) the Wasila and excellency, and raise him up in a praiseworthy position which You have promised', he will be assured of my intercession."* (Bukhâri)

## *Iqâmat*

*Iqâmat* is the second call to *Ṣalât* (prayer) and is uttered immediately before the beginning of the obligatory prayer offered with congregation.

**Text of *Iqâmat*:**

| | |
|---|---|
| *Allâhu Akbar, Allâhu Akbar,* | اللهُ أَكْبَرُ، اللهُ أَكْبَرُ. |
| Allâh is the Greatest, Allâh is the Greatest. | |
| *Ash hadu an-lâ ilâha illal lâh.* | أَشْهَدُ أَنْ لَا إِلٰهَ إِلَّااللهُ. |
| I bear witness that there is no deity but Allâh. | |
| *Ash hadu an-na Muḥammadar Rasûlul-lâh,* | أَشْهَدُ أَنَّ مُحَمَّدًا رَسُولُ اللهِ. |
| I bear witness that Muḥammad (ﷺ) is Allâh's Messenger. | |
| *Ḥayya 'alaṣ ṣalâh. Ḥayya 'alal falâḥ.* | حَيَّ عَلَى الصَّلَاةِ. حَيَّ عَلَى الْفَلَاح |
| Come to the Prayer. Come to your good. | |
| *Qad qâmatiṣ .ṣalâh, Qad qâmatiṣ .ṣalâh.* | قَدْ قَامَتِ الصَّلَاةُ، قَدْ قَامَتِ الصَّلَا |
| *Jamâ'at* is ready, *Jamâ'at* is ready. | |
| *Allâhu Akbar, Allâhu Akbar.* | اللهُ أَكْبَرُ ، اللهُ أَكْبَرُ |
| Allâh is the Greatest, Allâh is the Greatest. | |
| *lâ ilâha illal lâh.* | لَا إِلٰهَ إِلَّا اللهُ |
| There is no deity but Allâh. | |

This text of *Iqâmat* is the same as that mentioned in the *Ḥadith* of 'Abdullâh bin Zaid bin Abd Rabbihi who was the first to have a vision about *Adhân*.

Chapter 4

# Conduct of *Ṣalât* (Prayer)

## *Sutra*

Before a person starts to pray, he should place something at a short distance in front of him of the place where he prostrates (does *Sajdah*). Such an object is called *Sutra* and is used when the person is praying alone. A person passing in front of the person in *Ṣalât* (prayer), should pass on the outside of the *Sutra*.

If someone is praying in congregation, then the *Imâm* acts as the *Sutra*. The *Imâm*, however, must have his own individual *Sutra* in front of him.

## *Qiblah*

Wherever a person is in the world, he should face towards the *Ka'bah* when he is going to pray. The *Ka'bah* is in sacred mosque of Makkah in Saudi Arabia. Facing towards *Qiblah* (*Ka'bah*) is a very important condition of performing of *Ṣalât* (prayer). However, if the person is in a place such as a desert, jungle, unknown strange city or a place where he does not know the direction of the *Qiblah*, he should try his best to find out the direction of *Qiblah* from others. However, if it is not possible then he should use his judgment and face in a direction which he thinks is that of *Qiblah* and Allâh will accept his *Ṣalât* (prayer).

It is important to start the *Ṣalât* (prayer) facing the direction of *Qiblah* and it does not matter if his direction changes while he is praying e.g. in a ship, a train or an aeroplane etc.

***Note:*** Nowadays, a compass is available which gives the direction of *Qiblah*. In strange places and aeroplanes it is a useful instrument to possess.

## *Intention (Niyat)*

After facing the *Qiblah,* the person should make *Niyat* (intention). The intention is made within his mind, so the person should think about the particular obligatory, optional or *Nafl* prayer he intends to perform. He should not utter the words of *Niyat* aloud, as this is not authentic of approved by the Prophet (ﷺ).

## *Takbir Taḥrimah*

After making *Niyat* the person should start his *Ṣalât* (prayer) saying "*Allâhu Akbar*" (Allâh is the Greatest) raising both of his hands to the shoulders, with fingers stretching to the earlobes. He should then fold his hands over his chest right hand over the left hand. This first "*Allâhu Akbar*" is called *Takbir Taḥrimah* because after saying *Takbir Taḥrimah* every common and worldly action, talk or movement is forbidden. Throughout the *Ṣalât* (prayer) the eyes of the worshipper should point to the spot where the forehead rests in *Sajdah.*

**Where should the Hands be folded & placed after saying *Takbir Taḥrimah*?**

Some people place their hands under the navel, others place them under the chest but there are *Aḥâdith* which state that Prophet Muḥammad (ﷺ) used to place his hands over his chest.

a) Halb Ataee (رضي الله عنه) reported: "I saw the Prophet (ﷺ) placing his right hand over his left hand over his chest." (Aḥmad, Tirmidhi)

b) Wâ'il bin Ḥajr (رضي الله عنه) said: "I prayed with Prophet Muḥammad (ﷺ) and he put his right hand over his left hand over his chest." (Ibn Khuzaimah, Abu Dâwûd and Muslim)

There are some other narrations which state that some *Fuqhâ* used to place their hands under the chest but above the navel. Placing the hands in either of these positions is correct but it is better to place them over the chest according to the practice of Prophet Muḥammad (ﷺ) as mentioned in the above authentic *Aḥâdith.*

**Recitation before *Fâtiḥah:***

There are several *Du'â* which Prophet Muḥammad (ﷺ) used to recite before *Fâtiḥah*. We will mention two of them:

- «اللَّهُمَّ بَاعِدْ بَيْنِي وَبَيْنَ خَطَايَايَ كَمَا بَاعَدْتَ بَيْنَ الْمَشْرِقِ وَالْمَغْرِبِ، اللَّهُمَّ نَقِّنِي مِنْ خَطَايَا كَمَا يُنَقَّى الثَّوْبُ الأَبْيَضُ مِنَ الدَّنَسِ، اللَّهُمَّ اغْسِلْنِي مِن خَطَايَايَ بِالْمَآءِ والثَّلْجِ وَالْبَرَدِ» (بخاري و مسلم)

*"Allâhumma bâ'id baynee wa bayna khatâyâya kamâ bâ'adta baynal mashriqi wal maghribi. Allâhumma naqqinee min khatâyâ kamâ yunaq-qath thawbul abyaḍu minad-danasi. Allâhum-maghsilnee min khatâyâya bil mâ'i wath-thalji wal baradi."*

"O Allâh set me apart from my sins as east and west are apart from each other. O Allâh, cleanse me from sins as a white garment is cleansed from the dirt after thorough washing. O Allâh, wash me off from my sins with water, snow and hail."

If a person does not know the *Du'â* just mentioned then he should recite the following one. 'Umar (رضي الله عنه) is reported to have used this *Du'â* after saying *Takir Taḥrimah*:

- «سُبْحَانَكَ اللَّهُمَّ وَبِحَمْدِكَ وَتَبَارَكَ اسْمُكَ وَتَعَالَى جَدُّكَ وَلَا إِلَهَ غَيْرُكَ»

*"Subḥânaka Allâhumma wa biḥamdika watabâra kasmuka wata'âla jadduka wala ilâha ghayruka."*

"Glory be to You, O Allâh, and all praises are due unto You, and blessed is Your Name and high is Your Majesty and none is worthy of worship but You."

A person can read both *Du'â*, together or just one of them or any of the other *Du'â* which are approved by Prophet Muḥammad (ﷺ), and these are about 7. These *Du'â* can be found in different places of several books of *Ḥadith*, e.g. Muslim, Tirmidhi, Musnad-e- Imâm Aḥmad, Abu Dâwûd, Dâr-qutni, Nasâi, Ibn Mâjah, Ibn Hibbân and Muaṭṭa Imâm Mâlik.

All of the 7 *Du'â* can be read together before reciting *Surah Fâtiḥah.*

This recitation is called *Du'â-ul-Istiftâḥ* which means *Du'â* of starting *Du'â-ul-Istiftâḥ* should only by recited in the first *Rak'at.*

## *Ta'awwudh*

Then the person who is praying should say:

«أَعُوذُ بِاللهِ مِنَ الشَّيْطَانِ الرَّجِيمِ»

*"A'ûdhu bil-lâhi minash Shaytâ nir-rajeem"*

"I seek Allâh's protection from Satan who is accursed."

This should only be said in the first *Rak'at.*

## *Tasmiyah*

Then the person who is praying should say:

«بِسْمِ اللهِ الرَّحْمَنِ الرَّحِيمِ»

*"Bismillâh hir-Raḥmân ir-Raḥeem."*

"In the Name of Allâh, the Most Gracious, and the Most Merciful."

This should be said in every *Rak'at* before reciting *Surah Fâtiḥah.*

### *Surah Fâtiḥah*:

Then the person praying should recite *Surah Fâtiḥah*:

﴿ٱلْحَمْدُ لِلَّهِ رَبِّ ٱلْعَٰلَمِينَ ۝٢ ٱلرَّحْمَٰنِ ٱلرَّحِيمِ ۝٣ مَٰلِكِ يَوْمِ ٱلدِّينِ ۝٤ إِيَّاكَ نَعْبُدُ وَإِيَّاكَ نَسْتَعِينُ ۝٥ ٱهْدِنَا ٱلصِّرَٰطَ ٱلْمُسْتَقِيمَ ۝٦ صِرَٰطَ ٱلَّذِينَ أَنْعَمْتَ عَلَيْهِمْ غَيْرِ ٱلْمَغْضُوبِ عَلَيْهِمْ وَلَا ٱلضَّآلِّينَ﴾ آمين۔

*"Alḥamdu lil-lâhi rab-bil 'âlameen. Ar Raḥmân ir-Raḥeem. Mâliki yawmid-deen. Iyyaka na'budu wa iyyaka nasta'een. Ihdinas Ṣirâtal mustaqeem. Ṣirâtal ladheena an'amta 'alayhim. Ghayril maghdûbi 'alayhim walaḍ ḍâl-leen." Âmeen.*

"Praise in only for Allâh, Lord of the universe. The Most Kind, the Most Merciful. The Master of the Day of Judgment. You Alone we worship and to You Alone we pray for help. Show us the straight way, the way of those whom You have blessed. Who have not deserved Your Anger, nor gone astray." *Âmeen.*

Reciting *Fâtiḥah* is so important that Prophet Muḥammad (ﷺ) said that no prayer was acceptable without the recitation of *Fâtiḥah.*

a) 'Ubâdah bin Ṣâmit (رضي الله عنه) reported Allâh's Messenger (ﷺ) as saying: "There is no *Ṣalât* (prayer) acceptable without reciting *Surah Fâtiḥah.*" (Bukhâri, Muslim, Aḥmad, Abu Dâwûd, Tirmidhi, Nasâi & Ibn Mâjah)

b) Abu Hurairah (رضي الله عنه) reported that Allâh's Messenger (ﷺ) was saying that anyone who prayed any kind of *Ṣalât* (prayer) and did not read in that, *Umm-ul-Qur'ân,* (and in one version, *Fâtiḥah-tul-Kitâb*), his prayer will be deficient, will be deficient, will be deficient, and not complete. (Bukhâri, Muslim, Aḥmad)

c) Abu Hurairah (رضي الله عنه) reported Allâh's Messenger (ﷺ) as saying: "No Ṣalât (prayer) will benefit a person who did not read in that Surah Fâtiḥah." (Ibn Khuzaimah, Ibn Ḥibbân and Aḥmad)

In the light of the above *Aḥâdith* we understand that *Surah Fâtiḥah* must be recited or read in every *Rak'at* of any type of *Ṣalât* (prayer).

**Recitation of *Surah Fâtiḥah* behind an *Imâm*:**

Some people are very confused whether they should or should not read *Surah Fâtiḥah* while praying in congregation. But there should not be any confusion in this matter as the following *Aḥâdith* very clearly answer the question:

a) 'Ubâdah bin Ṣâmit (رضي الله عنه) said: "We were behind the Prophet (ﷺ) in the *Fajr* prayer, and he recited a passage from the Qur'ân, but the recitation became difficult for him. Then when he finished he said, "Do you recite behind your *Imâm*?" We replied, "Yes, Allâh's Messenger (ﷺ)." Then Allâh's Messenger (ﷺ) said: "Do not recite anything (behind the *Imâm*) except *Fâtiḥah-tul-Kitâb* (*Surah Fâtiḥah*) because he who does not include it in his recitation in prayer, his *Ṣalât* is not valid." (Abu Dâwûd and Tirmidhi)

b)  Abu Hurairah (⁕) reported that Allâh's Messenger (⁕) said: "If anyone observes prayer (*Ṣalât*) in which he does not read *Umm-ul-Qur'ân* (*Fâtiḥah*), it is deficient, it is deficient, it is deficient, and not complete." It was said to Abu Hurairah: "What should we do when we are behind an *Imâm*?" He, (Abu Hurairah ⁕) replied, "Read it in silence ... " (Muslim)

**Âmeen:**

It is *Sunnah* to say *Âmeen* when a person finishes recitation of *Surah Fâtiḥah*. If he is praying alone, he should say "*Âmeen*" in silence and if he is praying with congregation behind an *Imâm*, then he should say *Âmeen* fairly loudly when the *Imâm* finishes saying the last verse of *Surah Fâtiḥah*. When saying *Âmeen*, the voice of the whole congregation should resound at the same time.

There are many *Aḥâdith* which prove that saying *Âmeen* aloud is *Sunnah* of the holy Prophet (⁕) and it was the regular practice of the companions. We will mention a few of these *Aḥâdith* here:

a)  Na'eem Al Mujammar said: "I prayed behind Abu Hurairah (⁕). He recited '*Bismillâh hir-Raḥmânir-Raḥeem*', then he recited *Surah Fâtiḥah*, and when he reached *walaḍ ḍâl-leen*, he said, "*Âmeen*" after it and the people behind him said *Âmeen* ... " (Bukhâri)

b)  Abu Hurairah (⁕) reported that Allâh's Messenger (⁕) said: "When the *Imâm* says *Ghayril maghḍûbi 'alayhim walaḍ ḍâl-leen*, all of you should say *Âmeen*, because the angels say *Âmeen* and the *Imâm* says *Âmeen*. And whosoever say *Âmeen* and his voice blends with that of the angels he would be forgiven his sins." (Aḥmad, Abu Dâwûd & Nasâi)

c)  'Âisha (⁕) reported that Allâh's Messenger (⁕) said: "Jews are more envious of Muslims in two things: (a) our greeting someone with *Assalâmu 'alaykum,* and (b) saying *Âmeen* (aloud) behind the *Imâm.*" (Aḥmad and Ibn Mâjah)

d) Atâ said: "I found 200 of the companions praying in the mosque of the Prophet (ﷺ) and when the *Imâm* said *walaḍ ḍâl-leen,* I heard the echo of their voices resound with *Âmeen.*"

**Recitation after *Surah Fâtiḥah*:**

It is *Sunnah* for a person who is praying that he should read a *Surah* from Qur'ân after *Fâtiḥah* in the first two *Rak'at* of the *Farḍ* prayer. He can recite one or more *Surah*. Here are a few short *Surah* which you can recite:

a) ***Surah Ikhlâṣ*:**

بِسْمِ اللهِ الرَّحْمٰنِ الرَّحِيْم

﴿قُلْ هُوَ ٱللَّهُ أَحَدٌ ۝١ ٱللَّهُ ٱلصَّمَدُ ۝٢ لَمْ يَلِدْ وَلَمْ يُولَدْ ۝٣ وَلَمْ يَكُن لَّهُۥ كُفُوًا أَحَدٌۢ ۝٤﴾

*"Qul huwal lâhu aḥad. Allâhuṣ-Ṣamad. Lam yalid wa lam yûlad. Wa lam yakun-lahu kufuwan 'aḥad."*

"Say: He is Allâh, the only one. Allâh helps and does not need help. He does not produce a child, and He was not born of anyone. There is no one equal to Him."

b) ***Surah Falaq*:**

بِسْمِ اللهِ الرَّحْمٰنِ الرَّحِيْم

﴿قُلْ أَعُوذُ بِرَبِّ ٱلْفَلَقِ ۝١ مِن شَرِّ مَا خَلَقَ ۝٢ وَمِن شَرِّ غَاسِقٍ إِذَا وَقَبَ ۝٣ وَمِن شَرِّ ٱلنَّفَّـٰثَـٰتِ فِى ٱلْعُقَدِ ۝٤ وَمِن شَرِّ حَاسِدٍ إِذَا حَسَدَ ۝٥﴾

*"Qul a'ûdhu bi rab-bil falqa. Min shar-rimâ khlaq. Wa min shar-ri ghâsiqin idha waqab. Wa min shar-rin naf-fâthâti fi 'uqad. Wa min shar-ri ḥâsidin idha ḥasad."*

"Say: I seek refuge in the Lord of the dawn, from the evil of all that He has created, and from the evil of the darkness of night when it falls, and from the evil of those (charmers) who blow into knots. And from the evil of the envier when he envies."

c) ***Surah Nâs***:

بِسْمِ اللهِ الرَّحْمٰنِ الرَّحِيْم

﴿قُلْ أَعُوذُ بِرَبِّ ٱلنَّاسِ ۝١ مَلِكِ ٱلنَّاسِ ۝٢ إِلَٰهِ ٱلنَّاسِ ۝٣ مِن شَرِّ ٱلْوَسْوَاسِ ٱلْخَنَّاسِ ۝٤ ٱلَّذِى يُوَسْوِسُ فِى صُدُورِ ٱلنَّاسِ ۝٥ مِنَ ٱلْجِنَّةِ وَٱلنَّاسِ﴾

*"Qul a'ûdhu bi rab-bin nâs. Malikin nâs. Ilâ hin- nâs. Min shar-ril waswâ sil khan-nâs. Alladhi yuwaswisu fee ṣudû rin-nâs. Minal jin-nati wan- nâs."*

"Say: I seek refuge in the Sustainer of mankind. The Owner of mankind, Lord of mankin. From the evil of the sneaking whisperer. Who whispers in the hearts of mankind. (Whether he be) from among jinns or mankind."

## *Rukû' (Bowing)*

Then the person praying should say "*Allâhu Akbar*" raising both his hands to shoulder level with the palms facing outwards and fingers stretching to earlobes. He should then bend in *Rukû'* so that his trunk (i.e. from head to hips) becomes perpendicular to the rest of the body. His hands should rest on his knees with the fingers spread apart, taking care that his arms do not touch his body. The person should be calm and composed in the *Rukû'* posture and not hurry it. Then he should read at least three times:

«سُبْحَانَ رَبِّيَ الْعَظِيم»

*"Subḥâna Rab-bi yal 'Aẓeem"*

"Glory be to my Lord Who is the very Greatest." (He can read it 3, 5, 7, 9 or 11 etc. times)

There are some other *Du'â* Which can be read with *Subḥâna Rab-bi yal 'Aẓeem* or instead of *Subḥâna Rab-bi yal 'Aẓeem*. Two of them are mentioned below:

**Other *Du'â* in *Rukû'*:**

'Âisha (رضي الله عنها) reported that Allâh's Messenger (ﷺ) mostly read the following *Du'â* in his *Rukû'* and *Sajdah*:

«سُبْحَانَكَ اللَّهُمَّ رَبَّنَا وَبِحَمْدِكَ، اللَّهُمَّ اغفِرْ لِي» (البخاري و مسلم)

*"Subḥânaka Allâhumma Rab-banâ wa biḥamdika, Allâhum-maghfirlee"*

"Glory be to You, oh our Lord and all praise be to you. Oh Allâh, forgive me." (Bukhâri and Muslim)

Ali (رضي الله عنه) reported that Allâh's Messegner used to read the following *Du'â* in *Rukû'*:

«اللَّهُمَّ لَكَ رَكَعتُ وَبِكَ آمَنْتُ وَلَكَ اَسْلَمْتُ أَنْتَ رَبِّي خَشِعَ سَمْعِي وَبَصَرِي وَمُخِّي وَعَظْمِي وَعَصَبِي. وَمَا اسْتَقَلَّتْ بِهِ قَدَمَيَّ للهِ رَبِّ الْعَالَمِيْنَ» (أحمد، مسلم و أبو داود)

*"Allâhhumma laka raka'tu, wa bika âmantu, wa laka aslamtu, anta Rab-bi khashi'a sam'ee wa basaree wa mukh-khee wa 'aẓmee wa 'asabee. Wa masta qal-lat bihi qada may-ya lil-lâhi Rab-bil 'âlameen."*

"Oh! My Lord, I bowed to You and I believed in You and I submitted to You. You are my Lord. My ear, my sight, my brain, my bones, my tendons and whatever has been carried by my feet is submitted for the Lord of the worlds." (Aḥmad, Muslim and Abû Dâwûd etc.)

There are other *Du'â* which Prophet Muḥammd (ﷺ) read in *Rukû'* and they can be found in other books of *Ḥadith*.

**Perfection of *Rukû'* and *Sajdah*:**

Abi Mas'ud al Badri (ﷺ) reported that Allâh's Messenger (ﷺ) said:

> "Allâh does not consider the *Ṣalât* (prayer) of a man who does not straighten his back when bowing for *Rukû'* and performing *Sajdah.*" (Ibn Khuzaimah, Ibn Ḥibbân and Tabarâni)

Abi Qatâdah (ﷺ) reported that Allâh's Messenger (ﷺ) said: "The worst thief in one who steals in his *Ṣalât* (prayer)." Then the companions asked, "How can someone steal from his *Ṣalât* (prayer)?" Prophet (ﷺ) answered, "He does not complete his *Rukû'* and *Sajdah* with perfection." Or he said, "He does not make his back straight in *Rukû'* and *Sajdah.*" (Aḥmad, Ṭabarâni, Ibn Khuzaimah and Ḥâkim)

These *Aḥâdith* prove that *Rukû'* and *Sajdah* should be done calmly, slowly and perfectly, otherwise *Ṣalât* of the person will be deficient.

## *Qawmah (Standing afte Rukû')*

After the perfect *Rukû'*, the person praying should raise his head from *Rukû'* saying:

«سَمِعَ اللهُ لِمَنْ حَمِدَهُ»

*"Sami 'Allâhu liman ḥamidah."*

"Verily, Allâh listens to one who praises Him."

And[1] raise his hands up to the level of his shoulders with palms facing outwards and fingers stretched to the earlobes, and then he should lower

[1] Some people get very annoyed when they see someone raising his hands while going into *Rukû'* and again raising his hands while lifting his head from *Rukû'*.

There are, however, authentic *Aḥâdith* which prove that Prophet Muḥammad (ﷺ) used to raise his hands at the beginning of *Ṣalât* (prayer), before and after *Rukû'* and when standing up for the third *Rak'at*. Every single book of his hands to his sides. In the standing position, he should be erect so that the joints of his body go back in place. While in this position, he should recite one or all of the Following *Du'â* as many times as he likes.

***Du'â* in *Qawmah*:**

«رَبَّنَا وَلَكَ الْحَمْدُ»

a) *"Rab-banâ wa lakal ḥamd..."*

"Oh, our Lord, all the praises be to You."

«رَبَّنَا وَلَكَ الْحَمْدُ حَمْدًا كَثِيرًا طَيِّبًا مُبَارَكًا فِيهِ»

b) *"Rab-banâ wa lakal ḥamd, ḥamdan katheeran tayyiban mubârakan fihi."*

"Oh our Lord, all praises be to You, very many, pure and blessed praises be to You."

c) Abu Sa'eed Al-Khudree (ﷺ) says that when Allâh's Messenger (ﷺ) used to say: *"Sami 'Allâhu liman ḥamidah"*, he would follow it with:

«اللَّهُمَّ رَبَّنَا وَلَكَ الْحَمْدُ مِلْأَ السَّمٰوَاتِ وَمِلْأَ الْأَرْضِ وَمِلْأَ مَا شِئْتَ مِنْ شَيْءٍ بَعْدُ أَهْلَ الثَّنَآءِ وَالْمَجْدِ أَحَقُّ مَا قَالَ الْعَبْدُ وَكُلُّنَا لَكَ عَبْدٌ اللَّهُمَّ لَا مَانِعَ لِمَا أَعْطَيْتَ وَلَا مُعْطِيَ لِمَا مَنَعْتَ وَلَا يَنْفَعُ ذَا الْجَدِّ مِنْكَ الْجَدُّ» (مسلم، أحمد وأبو داود)

---

*Ḥadith* like Bukhâri, Muslim, Muaṭṭâ Imâm Mâlik, Abu Dâwûd, Tirmidhi, Nasâi, Ibn Mâjah, Ibn Khuzaimah, Hâkim, Aḥmad, Shâfa'ee Tabarâni, Baihaqi etc., mentions these *Aḥâdith*. Nearly four hundred companions also narrate this practice of Prophet Muḥammad (ﷺ). So, there is not the slightest doubt that the raising of hands is *Sunnat* and a person who practices this *Sunnat* gets a greater reward than the person who does not practice it. However, even though the action is mentioned in the *Aḥâdith*, all the *'Ulama* agree that the *Ṣalât* (prayer) of a person who does not raise his hands is acceptable. Therefore, Muslims should not fight over this issue. If someone does not wish to raise his hands, he should not discourage others from doing so because it is not a major controversial point.

> *"Allâhhumma Rab-banâ wa lakal ḥamdu mil'as samâwâti wa mil'al arḍi wa mil'a mâ shi'ta min shay'in ba'du: ah lath thanâ'e wal majdi aḥaq-qu mâ qâlal 'abdu wa kulluna laka 'abd. Allâhumma lâ mâni'a limâ a'tayta walâ mu'tiya limâ mana'ta walâ yanfa'u dhal jad-di minkal jad."* (Muslim, Aḥmad and Abu Dâwûd)
>
> "Oh Allâh, our Lord, all praises be to You, as much as they can fill the heavens and the earth and everything which You want to be filled after that. You deserve to be praised and glorified. You deserve more than what Your servant has said and all of us are Your slaves. Nobody can prevent whatever You want to give and nobody can give whatever You want to prevent and a person with high rank cannot benefit himself or another from his high rank against Your Will."

There are some other *Du'â* which can be read in the *Qawmah* position and these can be found in other books of *Ḥadith*.

## *First Sajdah (Prostration)*

After the perfect *Qawmah* the person praying should move to perform *Sajdah* saying:

*"Allâhu Akbar"* putting palms downwards on the ground below the ears. The knees should be brought downwards on the ground. His fingers and toes should be pointing towards *Qiblah* without spreading the fingers of the hands. During prostration seven parts of the body should touch the ground.

i) The forehead along with the tip of the nose. ii) both hands iii) both knees, iv) the bottom surface of the toes of both feet. In this position, he should say:

«سُبْحَانَ رَبِّيَ الأَعْلَى»

*"Subḥâna Rabbi yal a'la"*

"Oh Allâh, glory be to You, the Most High."

He should say this at least 3 times or 5, 7, 9, 11 etc. times.

There are some other *Du'â* which can be read in the *Sajdah* position.

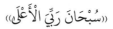

**Other *Du‘â* in *Sajdah*:**

i) Ali (﷠) said that Allâh's Messenger (ﷺ) used to say while doing *Sajdah*.

«اللَّهُمَّ لَكَ سَجَدْتُ وَبِكَ آمَنْتُ وَلَكَ أَسْلَمْتُ سَجَدَ وَجْهِي لِلَّذِي خَلَقَهُ وَصَوَّرَهُ فَأَحْسَنَ صُوَرَهُ وَشَقَّ سَمْعَهُ وَبَصَرَهُ فَتَبَارَكَ اللهُ أَحْسَنُ الْخَالِقِينَ» مسلم

*"Allâhhumma laka sajadtu, wa bika âmantu, walaka aslamtu, sajda wajhiya lilladhi khalaqahu wa saw-warahu fa aḥsana suwarahu, wa shaq-qa sam‘ahu wa basarahu fatabâra kal-lâhu aḥsanul khâliqeen."*

"Oh Allâh, for You I have prostrated, and in You I have faith, and unto You I have submitted, my forehead has prostrated in front of one Who created it and gave shape to it and made it perfectly. Then He gave power of hearing and sight, and blessed is Allâh's Name Who is the Perfect Creator." (Aḥmad and Muslim)

ii) Abu Hurairah (﷠) said that Allâh's Messenger (ﷺ) used to say in his *Sajdah*:

«اللَّهُمَّ اغْفِرْ لِي ذَنْبِي كُلَّهُ دِقَّهُ وَجِلَّهُ أَوَّلَهُ وَآخِرَهُ وَعَلَانِيَّتَهُ وَسِرَّهُ» (مسلم)

*"Allâhhum maghfirlee dhanbee kul-lahu diq-qahu, wa jil-lahu wa aw-walahu wa âkhirahu, wa ‘ala niy-yatahu wa sir-rahu."*

"Oh Allâh, forgive all of my sins, minor ones and major ones, ones I committed previously and ones I commit in the future, ones I commit openly and ones I commit secretly." (Muslim, Abu Dâwûd and Hakim)

There are some other *Du‘â* which Allâh's Messenger (ﷺ) used to say in his *Sajdah* but these *Du‘â* are too long to mention here. They can be found in authentic books of Ḥadith like Muslim, Aḥmad, Nasâi, Abu Dâwûd etc. It is not surprising that Prophet Muḥammad (ﷺ) stayed in *Rukû‘* and *Sajdah* for long intervals.

All of the authentically approved *Du‘â* can be said with *Subḥâna Rabbi yal a'la* or on their own or altogether according to the time available ane capacity of the person.

In *Sajdah* positon the worshipper is at his closest to Allâh. Hence, *Sajdah* should be performed calmly, and quietly, without fidgeting, and the worshipper should try to read as many *Du'â* as he possibly can.

## Jalsah (Sitting between two Sajdah)

After performing one *Sajdah* perfectly and calmly, the person praying should raise his head from *Sajdah* saying "*Allâhu Akbar*", bending the left foot and sitting on it while keeping the right foot propped up with its toes pointing towards the *Qiblah*, the palms of his hands should rest on his thighs and knees, the back should be straight so that the joints go back in place. It is *Sunnat* to say the following *Du'â* while sitting in between the two *Sajdah*:

«اللَّهُمَّ اغْفِرْ لِي وَارْحَمْنِيْ وَاهْدِنِيْ وَعَافِنِيْ وَارْزُقْنِيْ وَاجْبُرْنِي وَارْفَعْنِيْ»

"*Allâhhum maghfirlee warḥamnee wahdinee wa 'âfinee warzuqne, wajburnee war fa'nee*" (Abu Dâwûd)

"Oh Allâh, forgive me, and have mercy on me, and keep me on the right path, and keep me healthy, and provide me with Ḥalâl sources of living, and complete my shortcomings, and make my rank high."

The worshipper can say this *Du'â* once or as many times as he likes.

## Second Sajdah:

Then the person should perform the second *Sajdah* saying "*Allâhu Akbar*" and repeat what he did in the first *Sajdah*.

### Jalsah-e-Istarâḥat (Sitting for rest):

Then he should raise his head up saying "*Allâhu Akbar*" and sit for a short while as he did in *Jalsah*. He does this before standing up for the second *Rak'at*.

### Second Rak'at:

After standing up for the second *Rak'at*, he should fold his hands over his chest as he did in the first *Rak'at* and start his recitation by reading "*Bismillâh*... and *Surah Fâtiḥah* followed by any passage or a chapter or achapter of the holy Qur'ân." Then he should complete his second *Rak'at* in the manner of the first one.

While choosing a passage or a chapter for the recitation in the second or a subsequent *Rak'at,* the worshipper should observe the order in which they occur in the Holy Qur'ân. Also, each *Surah* or verse should be shorter than the one recited before it. Hence, longer *Surah* are recited before shorter *Surah*.

## *Tashahud*

After completing the last *Sajdah* of the second *Rak'at,* the person should raise his head saying: "*Allâhu Akbar*". He should sit as he sat between the two *Sajdah,* putting his left hand on his left knee and right hand on his right knee. The fist of the right hand is closed except for the index finger which is protruded. It is protruded so that the right thumb is brought to the second division of the index finger. In this position the person should read:

«التَّحِيَّاتُ لِلّٰهِ، وَالصَّلَوَاتُ والطَّيِّبَاتُ، السَّلَامُ عَلَيْكَ أَيُّهَاالنَّبِيُّ وَرَحْمَةُ اللهِ وَبَرَكَاتُهُ، السَّلَامُ عَلَيْنَا وَعَلَى عِبَادَ اللهِ الصَّالِحِينَ، أَشْهَدُ أَن لَا إِلٰهَ إِلَّا اللهُ، وَأَشْهَدُ أَنَّ مُحَمَّدًا عَبْدُهُ وَرَسُولُهُ» (متفق عليه)

> *"At-taḥiy-yâtu lil-lâhi was ̣salawâtu waṭ-tay yibâtu. As-salâmu 'alayka ay-yuhan-nabiy-yu wa raḥma tullâhi wa barakâtuhu, as-salâmu 'alaynâ wa 'ala 'ibâdil-lâ hiṣ-̣saliheen. Ash hadu an-lâ ilâha illallâhu wa ash hadu an-na Muḥammadan 'ab-duhu wa Rasûluhu."*
>
> "All the compliments, prayers and good things ae due to Allâh; peace be on you, O Prophet, and Allâh's Mercy and Blessings be on you. Peace be on us and on the true pious devotees of Allâh.

I testify that none has the right to be worshipped but Allâh, and I testify that Muḥammad (ﷺ) is His slave and His Messenger." (Agreed upon)

While reading "*Ash hadu... 'abduhu wa Rasûluhu*" a person should raise the index finger of his right hand slightly and return it to its previous position after he has finished saying it.

A person pryaing 2 *Rak'at* only should continue to the next stage which is *Ṣalât 'alan-Nabi* (*Darûd*).

**Standing up for Third *Rak'at*:**

If a person is praying three or four *Rak'at*, then he should stand up after *Tashahud* saying "*Allâhu Akbar*" and raising his hands, as he did in *Takbir Taḥrimah*, start his recitation with "*Bismillâh*... and then *Surah Fâtiḥah.*" In the third or fourth *Rak'at* of *Farḍ* prayer, recitation of *Fâtiḥah* is sufficient. There is no need to say another *Surah*. But a person praying *Sunnat* or *Nafl* prayer can read a *Surah* after *Fâtiḥah*. After recitation he should continue to complete his third *Rak'at* (or fourth *Rak'at* if he is praying four).

After the completion of last *Rak'at* he should sit for *Tashahud* as described above (as he sat after praying 2 *Rak'at*).

## *Ṣalât 'Alan-Nabi (Darûd)*

After *Tashahud,* he should read *Ṣalât 'alan-Nabi* (*Darûd*) as follows:

«اللَّهُمَّ صَلِّ عَلَى مُحَمَّدٍ وَ عَلَى آلِ مُحَمَّدٍ كَمَا صَلَّيْتَ عَلَى إِبْرَاهِيمَ وَعَلَى آلِ إِبْرَاهِيمَ، إِنَّكَ حَمِيدٌ مَجِيدٌ، اللَّهُمَّ بَارِكْ عَلَى مُحَمَّدٍ وَعَلَى آلِ مُحَمَّدٍ كَمَا بَارَكْتَ عَلَى إِبْرَاهِيمَ وَعَلَى آلِ إِبْرَاهِيمَ إِنَّكَ حَمِيدٌ مَجِيدٌ»

*"Allâhumma sal-li 'ala Muḥammadin wa 'ala âli Muḥammadin, kamâ ṣal-layta 'ala Ibrâheema wa 'ala âli Ibrâheema innaka Ḥamidun Majid. Allâhumma bârik ala Muḥammadin wa 'ala âli Muḥammadin kamâ barakta ala Ibrâheema wa 'ala âli Ibrâheema Innaka Ḥamidun Majid."*

"Oh Allâh, send grace and honour on Muḥammad (ﷺ) and on the family and true followers of Muḥammad (ﷺ), just as You sent grace and honour on Ibrâheem (عليه السلام) and on the family and ture followers of Ibrâheem (عليه السلام) Surely, You are Praiseworthy, the Great. Oh Allâh, send Your blessings on Muḥammad (ﷺ) and the true followers of Muḥammad (ﷺ), just as You sent blessings on Ibrâheem (ﷺ) and his true followers. Surely, You are Praiseworthy, the Great."

**Du'â after *Ṣalât 'Alan-Nabi* (*Darûd*):**

There are quite a lot of *Du'â* which Prophet (ﷺ) used to say after *Darûd* and he taught them to the companions. Here we will mention a few of them:

i) 'Abdullâh bin 'Amr (رضي الله عنه) said that Abu Bakr (رضي الله عنه) said to Allâh's Messenger, "Please teach me a *Du'â* so I can say it in my *Ṣalât* (prayer)." So Allâh's Messenger (ﷺ) said, "Say:

«اللَّهُمَّ إِنِّيْ ظَلَمْتُ نَفْسِيْ ظُلْمًا كَثِيْرًا ، وَلَا يَغْفِرُ الذُّنُوْبَ إِلَّا أَنْتَ، فَاغْفِرْ لِيْ مَغْفِرَةً مِنْ عِنْدِكَ وَارْحَمْنِيْ إِنَّكَ أَنْتَ الْغَفُوْرُ الرَّحِيْمُ» (بخاري و مسلم)

*"Allâhumma innee ẓalamtu nafsee ẓulman katheeran – wa lâ yaghfi rudh dhunûba illâ Anta faghfirlee maghfiratam 'indika, war ḥamnee innaka antal Ghafûrur Raḥeem."* (Bukhâri & Muslim)

"Oh Allâh, I have been very cruel to myself (by ignoring my duty to You) and there is no one who can forgive the sins except You. So forgive me because You are the only Forgiver and have mercy on me. Verily, You are the Forgiver and Merciful."

ii) Shaddâd bin Aus (رضي الله عنه) reported that the Prophet of Allâh (ﷺ) used to say in his *Ṣalât* (prayer):

«اللَّهُمَّ إِنِّيْ أَسْئَلُكَ الثَّبَاتَ فِي الْأَمْرِ وَالْعَزِيْمَةَ عَلَى الرُّشْدِ وَأَسْئَلُكَ شُكْرَ نِعْمَتِكَ وَحُسْنَ عِبَادَتِكَ وَأَسْئَلُكَ قَلْبًا سَلِيْمًا وَلِسَانًا صَادِقًا وَأَسْئَلُكَ مِنْ خَيْرِ مَا تَعْلَمُ وَأَعُوْذُ بِكَ مِنْ شَرِّ مَا تَعْلَمُ وَاسْتَغْفِرُكَ لِمَا تَعْلَمُ» (نسائي)

*"Allâhumma innee as-'alu kath thabata fil amri, wal 'azeemata 'alar rushdi, wa as-'aluka shukra ni'matika, wa ḥusna 'ibâdatika, wa as-'aluka qalban saleeman-wa lisânan ṣâdiqan, wa as-'aluka min khayri mâ ta'lamu, wa a'udhubika min shar-ri mâ ta'lamu, wa as taghfiruka, limâ ta'lamu."*

"Oh Allâh, I ask You for strength in every matter of *Deen* and a strong will power to be on the right path. And I ask You to make me thankful for Your Bounties and give me ability to worship Your perfectly. And I ask You to make my heart sincere and my tongue truthful. I ask You for every goodness known to You and I seek refuge in You from everything bad that You know is bad. I ask Your Forgiveness for all mistakes You know." (Nasâi)

iii) 'Âisha (ﷺ) reported that the Prophet (ﷺ) used to say this *Du'â* in his *Ṣalât* (prayer):

«اللَّهُمَّ إِنِّي أَعُوذُ بِكَ مِنْ عَذَابِ الْقَبْرِ وَأَعُوذُ بِكَ مِنْ فِتْنَةِ الدَّجَّالِ، وَأَعُوذُ بِكَ مِنْ فِتْنَةِ الْمَحْيَا وَالْمَمَاتِ. اَللَّهُمَّ إِنِّي أَعُوذُ بِكَ مِنَ الْمَأْثَمِ وَالْمَغْرَمِ» (بخاري و مسلم)

*"Allâhumma innee a'ûdhubika min adhâbil qabri, wa a'ûdhubika min fitna tid daj-jâli, wa a'ûdhubika min fitna til maḥya wal mamât. "Allâhumma innee a'ûdhubika minal ma'thami wal maghrami."* (Bukhâri and Muslim)

"Oh Allâh I seek refuge in You from the punishment of the grave, and I seek refuge in You from the troubles of *Daj-jâl*, and I seek refuge in You from the difficulties and troubles of the life and death. Oh Allâh, I seek refuge in You from every kind of sin and unexpected troubles."

«رَبِّ اجْعَلْنِيْ مُقِيْمَ الصَّلوٰةِ وَمِنْ ذُرِّيَّتِيْ رَبَّنَا وَتَقَبَّلْ دُعَاءَ رَبَّنَا اغْفِرْ لِي وَلِوَالِدَيَّ وَلِلْمُؤْمِنِيْنَ يَوْمَ يَقُوْمُ الْحِسَابِ» (بخاري و مسلم)

*"Rab bij'alnee muqeemaṣ ṣalati wa min dhur-riy yatee rab-banâ wa taqab-bal du'â, rab-ba naghfirlee waliwaliday-ya wa lil mu'mineena yawma yaqûmul ḥisâb."*

"Oh Lord, make me and my children keep up *Ṣalât* (prayer). Our Lord, accept our *Du'â* (prayer). Our Lord, forgive me and my parents and all the believers on the Day of Judgment."

Although most people read *Rab bij'alnee* after *Darûd*; it is permitted to recite any nice *Du'â*. However, it should be known that this *Du'â* is not one of those *Du'â* which Prophet (ﷺ) used to say after *Darûd*. It is preferable to read both *Rab bij'a;mee* and the *Du'â* which are authentically proved from the Prophet (ﷺ) and those he taught to his companions. We have mentioned only four but there are about twelve. However, they are too lengthy to mention here.

**Ending the *Ṣalât* (Prayer):**

After praying for himself as much as the person wishes, he should end his *Ṣalât* (prayer) saying:

«السَّلَامُ عَلَيْكُمْ وَرَحْمَةُ اللهِ»

*"As-salâmu 'alaykum wa raḥmatul lâh"*

"Peace be on you and the Mercy of Allâh."

Turning the face first to the right and then to the left, both times over the shoulder. This brings the two, three or four *Rak'at* of the *Ṣalât* (prayer) to completion.

## *Du'â after Salutation*

There are many *Du'â* which Prophet Muḥammad (ﷺ) used to say after salutation. So, a person praying should try to memorise them and follow the practice of Prophet Muḥammad (ﷺ). Some of these *Du'â* we will mention here:

It was the continuous practice of Prophet Muḥammad (ﷺ) when he turned away from his *Ṣalât* (prayer) to say:

1. أ) اللهُ أَكْبَرُ.

ب) أَسْتَغْفِرُ اللهَ، أَسْتَغْفِرُ اللهَ، أَسْتَغْفِرُ اللهَ.

ج) اللَّهُمَّ أَنْتَ السَّلَامُ وَمِنكَ السَّلَامُ تَبَارَكْتَ يَا ذَا الجَلَالِ وَالإِكْرَامِ. (مسلم)

a) *"Allâhu Akbar"* (once aloud) "Allâh is the Greatest."

b) *"Astagh firul-lâh."* (3 times) "I ask Allâh to forgive me."

c) *"Allâhumma Antas-salâmu wa minkas salâmu, tabârakta yâ dhaljalâli wal ikrâm."*

"Oh Allâh, You are the peace, and You are the source of peace, You are blessed, O Possessor of glory and honour." (Muslim)

«اللَّهُمَّ أَعِنِّي عَلَى ذِكْرِكَ وَشُكْرِكَ وَحُسْنِ عِبَادَتِكَ»

2. *"Allâhumma a'innee 'ala dhikrika wa shukrika wa ḥusni 'ibadatika."* (Aḥmad and Abu Dâwûd)

"Oh Allâh, help me to remember You all the time, And to thank You, and to worship You perfectly."

«لاَ إِلَهَ إِلَّا اللهُ وَحْدَهُ لَا شَرِيكَ لَهُ، لَهُ الْمُلْكُ وَلَهُ الْحَمْدُ وَ هُوَ عَلَى كُلِّ شَيْءٍ قَدِيرٌ، اللَّهُمَّ لَا مَانِعَ لِمَا أَعْطَيْتَ وَلَا مُعْطِيَ لِمَا مَنَعْتَ وَلَا يَنْفَعُ ذَا الْجَدِّ مِنْكَ الْجَدُّ» (بخاري و مسلم)

3) *"Lâ ilâha illâl lâhu waḥdahu lâ shareeka lahu. Lahul mulku wala hul ḥamdu wa huwa 'alâ kul-li shay'in Qadeer. Allâhumma lâ mâni'a limâ a'tayta wa lâ mu'tiya limâ mana'ta wa lâ yanfa'u dhaljad-di minkal-jad."*

"There is no God but Allâh, He is the only One and has no partner, sovereignty and praise are only for Him, and He has full authority over everything.

Nobody can prevent whatever You want to give and nobody can give whatever You want to prevent and a person with high rank cannot benefit himself or another from his high rank against Your Will. (Bukhâri, Muslim)

سُبْحَانَ اللهِ (33 مرة) اَلْحَمْدُ للهِ (33 مرة) اللهُ أَكْبَرُ (34 مرة)

4) It is *Sunnat* to say: *Subḥân Allâh* (33 times), "Glory be to Allâh." *Alḥamdu lillâh* (33 times), "Praise be to Allâh." & *Allâhu Akbar* (34 times), "Allâh is the Greatest."

There are very many *Du'â* which Prophet Muḥammad (ﷺ) used to say and he taught them to his companions. These can be found in famous books of *Ḥadith*.

Chapter 5

# Occasional *Ṣalât* (Prayer)

## Witr (Prayer)

*Witr* prayer is *Sunnat Mu'akkadah.* It is very much emphasized by Prophet Muḥammad (ﷺ). He did not leave this *Ṣalât* (prayer) even during a journey or when mounted on camelback.

It was so much emphasized that some Muslim scholars understood that it was *Wajib* (compulsory) but after a careful study of *Aḥâdith* it can be said that it is not *Wajib* but a very much emphasized *Ṣalât* prayer.

*Witr* prayer is often mistakenly thought of as part of the *'Ishâ* prayer. This is not so. *Witr* prayer is a separate prayer which can be offered after the *'Ishâ* prayer right up to the break of dawn. For the convenience of the believers, Prophet (ﷺ) allowed *Witr* to be offered straight after *'Ishâ*. In Arabic the word *Witr* means: One. In *Aḥâdith* Allâh's Messenger (ﷺ) says:

> *"Allâh is One, so He likes the number one."* (Muslim)

Allâh also likes odd numbers because when an odd number is divided by 2, the remainder is always one. For this reason Prophet (ﷺ) preferred odd numbers. He liked to do things in odd numbers in his routing life also such as: when offering *Ṣalât,* saying *Du'â,* eating dates etc. That is why Prophet (ﷺ) asked the believers to pray *Witr* at the end of the night prayer so that it can make the night prayer into an odd number.

'Abdullâh bin 'Umar (رضي الله عنهما) says that Allâh's Messenger (ﷺ) said:

> *"Night prayer is to be offered in 2 Rak'at units. When one of you feels that dawn is near then he should offer 1 Rak'at which can make all the night prayer he offered into an odd number."* (Bukhâri & Muslim)

**Number of Rak'at of Witr prayer:**

'Abdullâh bin 'Umar (☺) said that Allâh's Messenger (☺) said: "*Witr* prayer is one *Rak'at* at the end of the *Nafl* prayer at night."

Abu Ayyûb (☺) says that Prophet Muḥammad (☺) said: "Every Muslim should pray *Witr*. Anyone who likes to pray 5 *Rak'at* of *Witr*, he should do so; anyone who likes to pray 3 *Rak'at*, he should do so; and anyone who likes to pray one *Rak'at*, he should do so." (Abu Dâwûd, Nasâi and Ibn Mâjah)

We understand from the above mentioned *Aḥâdith* that the actual *Witr* prayer is one *Rak'at*, although a person can offer, 1, 3, 5, 7 or 9 *Rak'at* of *Witr* prayer. All of these numbers are approved by Prophet Muḥammad (☺) in authentic *Aḥâdith*.

**Time of Witr prayer:**

*Witr* prayer can be offered the *'Ishâ* prayer right up to the break of dawn.

'Âisha (☺) said: "Prophet Muḥammad (☺) prayed *Witr* during all times of the night. Sometimes he prayed *Witr* during the first part of the night, sometimes during the middle part of the night, and sometimes during the end part of the night, but he used to complete the prayer before the break of dawn." (Bukhâri and Muslim)

However, a person who thinks he could not get up to pray *Witr* at the end part of the night, can offer *Witr* immediately after *'Ishâ* or before he goes to bed. But someone who thinks that he can get up and pray *Nafl* at night, should pray *Witr* at the end of his night prayer.

Jâbir (☺) said that the Prophet (☺) said: "Anyone of you who could not get up at the end part of the night, he should pray *Witr* in the first part of the night; and anyone of you who thinks he can get up at the end part of the night, he should pray *Witr* then, because the angels are present for the prayer offered at the end part of the night." (Muslim, Aḥmad, Tirmidhi and Ibn Mâjah)

**How to pray *Witr*:**

When praying one *Witr*, a person can offer it as the usual prayer.

When praying 3, 5, 7 or 9 *Rak'at* of *Witr* prayer, thers is more than one way the prayer can be offered. For example:

a) A person praying 3 *Rak'at Witr* can pray 2 *Rak'at* like the usual prayer. After the Salutation, *As-salâmu 'alaykum wa raḥmatul-lâh,* first to the right and then to the left, he should get up immediately to complete the third *Rak'at*. This way of offering *Witr* prayer is called *Witr bil faṣal'*.

b) A person praying 3 *Rak'at* or 5 *Rak'at Witr* should not sit for *Tashahud* in between the *Rak'at* except in the last *Rak'at.*

c) A person praying 3, 5 or 7 *Rak'at Witr* should sit in *Tashahud* in the last but one *Rak'at,* e.g. in the second *Rak'at* if he is offering 3 *Witr,* fourth *Rak'at* if he is offering 5 *Witr,* or sixth *Rak'at* if he is offering 7 *Witr* and so on. He should read *Tashahud* and then get up for the last *Rak'at* and complete it.

All 3 methods are authentic and are practiced by the great *'Ulamâ* and scholars. So Muslims can choose any one of these 3 methods to offer the *Witr* prayer. When praying 3 *Rak'at Witr,* however, it is preferable to choose method 'a' or 'b' as Prophet Muḥammad (ﷺ) said: "Do not make your *Witr* prayer similar to your *Maghrib* prayer." (Qiyâmul-lail)

***Du'â Qunût* in *Witr* prayer:**

Reading *Du'â Qunût* in the last *Rak'at* of the *Witr* prayer is a proved practice of Prophet Muḥammad (ﷺ) and it can be read before *Rukû'* or after *Rukû'.*

a) Someone who wants to read *Qunût* before *Rukû'*, he should read it after he has finished reciting *Surah Fâtiḥah* and chapter of the Holy Qur'ân. While reciting *Du'â Qunût,* a person can cup his hands in front of him or he can leave them folded.

b) Someone who wants to read *Du'â Qunût* after the *Rukû'*, he can read it with his hands cupped in front of him or he can let his hands rest at his sides. Saying *Du'â* after the *Rukû'* and cupping hands in front is preferable as this was the practice of Prophet Muḥammad (ﷺ).

Some *Fuqahâ'* insist that reading *Du'â Qunût* is compulsory in the last *Rak'at* of the *Witr* and some others say it is compulsory in the last *Rak'at* of the *Fajr* prayer, but if you study *Aḥâdith* carefully you will find that it is not compulsory either in the *Witr* or in the *Fajr* prayer. Therefore, if a person leaves *Du'â Qunût* in his *Witr* prayer, his prayer will not be deficient. Also, if someone does not know *Du'â Qunût*, he need not say another chapter of the Qur'ân or any other words in its replacement. *Du'â Qunût*, can be read in any *Ṣalât* (prayer).

**Text of *Du'â Qunût*:**

Hasan bin 'Ali (رضي الله عنهما) said that Allâh's Messenger (ﷺ) taught me the words which I should say in the *Du'â* or *Witr*:

a) «اللَّهُمَّ اهْدِنِيْ فِيمَنْ هَدَيْتَ وَعَافِنِيْ فِيمَنْ عَافَيْتَ وَتَوَلَّنِي فِيمَنْ تَوَلَّيْتَ وَبَارِكْ لِي فِيْمَا أَعْطَيْتَ وَقِنِيْ شَرَّ مَا قَضَيْتَ فَإِنَّكَ تَقْضِيْ وَلَا يُقْضَي عَلَيْكَ إِنَّهُ لَا يَذِلُّ مَنْ وَّالَيْتَ وَلَا يَعِزُّ مَنْ عَادَيْتَ تَبَارَكْتَ رَبَّنَا وَتَعَالَيْتَ نَسْتَغْفِرُكَ وَنَتُوبُ إِلَيْكَ وَصَلَّى اللهُ عَلَى النَّبِيِّ»

*"Allâhum mahdinee feeman hadayta, wa 'âfinee feeman 'âfayta, wa tawal-lanee feeman tawal-layta, wa bârik lee feemâ a'taita, wa qinee shar-ra mâ qaḍayta, fa-innaka taqḍee walâ yuqḍâ 'alayk, innahu lâ yadhil-lu manw wâlayta walâ ya'iz-zu man 'âdaita, tabârakta Rabbanâ wa ta 'âlaita, nastaghfiruka wa natubu ilayka, wa sal-lal lahu 'alan-nabee."* (Abu Dâwûd, Nasâi and Ibn Mâjah)

"Oh Allâh make me among those whom You have guided, and make me among those whom You have saved, and make me among those whom You have chosen, and bless whatever You have given me, and protect me from the evil which You have decreed; verily, You decide the things and nobody can decide against You; surely the person You befriended can't be disgracecd, and the person You opposed can't be honoured. You are Blessed, our Lord, and Exalted, we ask for Your Forgiveness and turn to You. Peace and Mercy of Allâh be upon the Prophet."

b) «اَللَّهُمَّ إِنَّا نَسْتَعِينُكَ وَنَسْتَغْفِرُكَ وَنُؤْمِنُ بِكَ وَنَتَوَكَّلُ عَلَيْكَ وَنُثْنِي عَلَيْكَ الْخَيْرَ وَنَشْكُرُكَ وَلَا نَكْفُرُكَ وَنَخْلَعُ وَنَتْرُكُ مَنْ يَفْجُرُكَ. اَللَّهُمَّ إِيَّاكَ نَعْبُدُ وَلَكَ نُصَلِّي وَنَسْجُدُ وَإِلَيْكَ نَسْعَىٰ وَنَحْفِدُ وَنَرْجُو رَحْمَتَكَ وَنَخْشَىٰ عَذَابَكَ إِنَّ عَذَابَكَ بِالْكُفَّارِ مُلْحَقٌ»

*"Allâhumma innâ nasta'eenuka wa nastaghfiruka wa nu'minu bika wa natawak-kalu 'alayka wa nuthnee 'alayk-al khayra. Wa nashkuruka wa lâ nakfuruka wa nakhla'u wa natruku man-yafjuruka. Allâhumma iyyâka na'budu wa laka nusal-lee wa nasjudu wa'ilayka nas'a wa naḥfidu wa narjû raḥmataka wa nakhsha 'adhâbaka inna 'adhâbaka bil kuf-fâri mulḥiqun."*

"Oh Allâh, we ask You for help and seek Your Forgiveness, and we believe in You and have trust in You, and we praise You in the best way and we thank You and we are not ungrateful to You, and we forsake and turn away from the one who disobesy You. O Allâh, we wirship You only and pray to You and prostrate ourselves before You, and we run towards Your and serve You, and we hope to receive Your Mercy, and we fear Your punishment. Surely, the disbelievers will receive Your punishment."

Some *'Umamâ* recommend this *Du'â* in the *Witr* prayer. Of course, it can be read as it is a nice *Du'â* but it is not one of those *Du'â* which Prophet Muḥammad (ﷺ) read in his *Qunût*.

There are some other *Du'â* which Prophet Muḥammad (ﷺ) used to read in his *Qunût* in the *Witr* prayer or in his other prayers.

A person can read all these *Du'â* together or just one of them or combine them with other *Du'â*.

# *Jum'ah* (Friday Prayer)

## *Importance of attending Friday prayer*

Friday prayer is very important in Islâm. It has got its own moral, social and political benefits. It is obligatory on every Muslim except women, children, slaves, seriously ill people and travelers. They can pray *Jum'ah* but it is not obligatory on them.

Prophet Muḥammad (ﷺ) has given a strong warning to a person who leaves his *Jum'ah* prayer without a good reason.

In one *Ḥadith* 'Abdullah bin Mas'ûd (رضي الله عنه) narrates what Allâh's Messenger (ﷺ) once said about the people who did not come to the Friday prayer without a good reason.

> *"I wish to appoint someone to lead the prayer and myself go the houses of those who missed the Friday prayer and set fire to their houses with the occupants in them."* (Muslim, Aḥmad)

Another *Ḥadith* states:

> *"A person who leaves 3 Friday prayers consecutively, Allâh puts a seal on his heart."* (Aḥmad, Tirmidhi and Abu Dâwûd)

**Importance of cleanliness for Friday prayer:**

Because in Friday prayer a comparatively large number of Muslims gather in a big place, so, Islâm emphasized on the physical cleanliness as well. Prophet (ﷺ) said:

> *"A person who has a bath on Friday, cleanses himself fully, uses oil and perfume; then goes to the mosque early in the afternoon and takes his place quietly without pushing or disturbing people; then he prays (optional prayer as much as he was able to pray); then sits quietly listening to the Khutbah, he will be forgiven his sins between this Jum'ah and the next Jum'ah."* (Bukhâri)

**Importance of going early to Friday prayer:**

On Friday it is more rewarding to get ready quickly to go to the mosque.

Abu Hurairah (ﷺ) narrated that Allâh's Messenger (ﷺ) said:

> *"On Friday the angels stand at the door of the mosque and write down the names of the people in the order in which they enter the mosque for Friday prayer. The first group of people who enter the mosque get the reward equivalent to that of sacrificing a camel, the people who enter the mosque after them get the reward equivalent to that of sacrificing a cow. The people who enter the mosque after them get the reward equivalent to that of sacrificing a ram and the people who follow on likewise get the reward of a chicken, egg and soon, there is a gradation of rewards for the people as they enter. The angels keep writing the names of the people as they enter the mosque until the Imâm sits down to give Khutbah. Then the angels collect their registers and sit and listen to the Khutbah."* (Bukhâri & Muslim)

***Ṣalât* (Prayer) before *Jum'ah*:**

A person who goes to attend Friday prayer can pray as many *Nafl* as he wishes after the sun has declined from its zenith to when the *Imâm* comes to give *Khutbah*. Anyhow he is expected to pray at least 2 *Rak'at Sunnat*.

**Listening to *Khutbah* (religious talk):**

Once the *Khutbah* starts, the whole congregation should listen to it in silence. If a person arrives while the *Imâm* is giving *Khutbah* then this person should pray 2 *Rak'at Nafl* before sitting down to listen to *Khutbah*.

Jâbir (ﷺ) said that Allâh's Messenger (ﷺ) said while he was giving *Khutbah*:

> *"If anyone of you goes to attend the Friday prayer while the Imâm is delivering Khutbah, he should pray 2 Rak'at and should not make them long."* (Muslim)

There is another *Ḥadith* Jâbir (ﷺ) says that once a man came to Friday prayer while Allâh's Messenger (ﷺ) was delivering *Khutbah*, so

Allâh's Messenger (ﷺ) asked him, "Did you pray?" "No", he answered. Then Prophet (ﷺ) said to him, "Stand up and pray." (Bukhâri, Muslim, Abu Dâwûd and Tirmidhi)

It is continuous practice in some mosques that those who arrive, while the *Imâm* is giving speech, sit down and listen to the speech. When the *Imâm* has finished the speech he gives time to the late arrivals to pray 2 or 4 *Rak'at Sunnat*. After that the *Imâm* gives a short *Khutbah* in Arabic before praying the *Jum'ah* prayer.

These people get very annoyed if they see a person offering 2 *Rak'at Sunnat* while the *Imâm* is giving speech. They feel that the person is being disrespectful to the *Imâm*. This is incorrect and unproved from the practice of Prophet Muḥammad (ﷺ). It is also against those *Aḥâdith* which we mentioned above and the one we are mentioning below. Abi Qatadah (ﷺ) says that Allâh's Messenger (ﷺ) said:

> *"Whenever one of you enters the mosque he should not sit down without offering 2 Rak'at."* (Bukhâri and Muslim)

These *Aḥâdith* clarify the points which are mispractised as above. The *Imâm* an *'Ulamâ* who have even a slight fear of Allâh and respect for *Ḥadith* and the *Sunnah* of Prophet Muḥammad (ﷺ), should stop this practice and should not become annoyed when others pray 2 *Rak'at*.

**Actual *Jum'ah* prayer:**

*Jum'ah* prayer is 2 *Rak'at Farḍ*. If a person is late and finds only 1 *Rak'at* with the congregation, he should complete the second *Rak'at* alone. If a person arrives so late that he misses the *Jum'ah* prayer completely then he has to ofter 4 *Rak'at Farḍ* and *Ẓuhr* prayer. The *Jum'ah* prayer is replacement of *Ẓuhr* prayer but the *Imâm* has to recite *Qira't* aloud in *Jum'ah* prayer.

***Ṣalât* (Prayer) after *Jum'ah*:**

After the *Jum'ah* prayer, 2 *Rak'at* of *Sunnat* prayer is an authentically proved practice of Prophet Muḥammad (ﷺ) but some companions used to pray 4 or 6 *Rak'at Sunnat* after the *Jum'ah* prayer.

Ibn 'Umar (ﷺ) says that Allâh's Messenger (ﷺ) did not pray after the Friday prayer until he went home and then he prayed 2 *Rak'at.* (Bukhari and Muslim)

Abu Hurairah (ﷺ) narrated that Allâh's Messenger (ﷺ) said:

> *"Anyone of you who is going to pray after the Friday prayer, he should pray 4 Rak'at."* (Muslim)

'Atâ says: Whenever 'Abdullâh bin 'Umar (ﷺ) prayed *Jum'ah* in Makkah, he would move a little forward after the *Jum'ah* prayer and offer 2 *Rak'at*; then he would move a little forward again and offer 4 *Rak'at.* And whenever he prayed *Jum'ah* in Al-Madina, he did not pray in the mosque after the *Jum'ah* prayer until he went back home; then he prayed 2 *Rak'at.* When he was asked why he did not pray in the mosque after the *Jum'ah* prayer. He answered, "This was the practice of Prophet Muḥammad (ﷺ)."

These *Aḥadith* clarify that 2, 4 or 6 *Rak'at* can be offered after the *Jum'ah* prayer according to the time and capacity of the person. It is not good practice to accuse people who read 2 *Rak'at* only because this, too, was the authentic practice of Prophet Muḥammad (ﷺ).

## *'Eid* Prayer

**Place for *'Eid* prayer:**

*'Eid* prayer should be offered outdoor in the open, e.g. in a park, field, or a desert etc. If it is wet or not possible to find a suitable outdoor place it can be prayed in a mosque or a large hall. (Abu Dâwûd)

**Time of *'Eid* prayer:**

*'Eid* prayer should be offered when the sun is obvious above the horizon.

**Number of *Rak'at* of *'Eid* prayer:**

*'Eid* prayer is 2 *Rak'at.* There is no *Nafl* prayer before or after the *'Eid* prayer. There is no *Iqâmat* or *Adhân* for *'Eid* prayer. Ibn Abbâs (ﷺ) reported: *"No doubt, Prophet Muḥammad (ﷺ) used to pray 2 Rak'at only for 'Eid prayer. He did not pray anything before or after that."* (Bukhâri & Muslim)

**Conduct of *'Eid* prayer:**

Two *Rak'at* of *'Eid* prayer should be offered in the same manner as the 2 *Rak'at* of the usual prayer except that there are 7 *Takbir* in the first *Rak'at* and 5 *Takbir* in the second *Rak'at.* With each extra *Takbir,* the hands should be raised up to the shoulder level (as in *Takbir Taḥrimah*).

All extra *Takbir* should be pronounced before starting *Qirâ't* (recitation).

Kathir bin 'Abdullâh reported from his father and his father from grandfather that Prophet (ﷺ) said 7 *Takbir* in the first *Rak'at* and 5 *Takbir* in the second *Rak'at* of *'Eid* prayer before beginning recitation. (Tirmidhi, Ibn Mâjah and Dârmi)

***'Eid* prayer is offered before *Khutbah*:**

Ja'far bin Muḥammad (رضي الله عنه) reported: "No doubt, Prophet Muḥammad (ﷺ), Abu Bakr (رضي الله عنه) and 'Umar (رضي الله عنه) said 7 extra *Takbir* in the first *Rak'at* of their *'Eid* and Rain Prayer and five extra *Takbir* in the second *Rak'at* of their *'Eid* and Rain Prayer. Prophet (ﷺ) offered *'Eid* prayer before *Khutbah* and recited aloud." (Shâfa'ee)

## *Janâzah* Prayer (Funeral Prayer)

It is a right of a Muslim that when he passes away, other Muslims should pray *Janâzah* prayer for him. *Janâzah* prayer is supererogatory prayer. If no one from the whold of the Muslim community prayed the *Janâzah* prayer; then the whole community would be considered sinful is the Sight of Allâh. If some of the people prayed the *Janâzah* prayer then the whole community is saved from the Anger of Allâh even though the reward will only be given to the participants only.

In *Aḥâdith* Prophet Muhammad (ﷺ) emphasized and encouraged the Muslims to attend funeral ceremonies. So, every Muslim male should try his best to fulfil his duty for the deceased. *Janâzah* prayer should be prayed in congregation as this is more rewardful. It can be prayed in more than one congregation but by different people.

*Janâzah* prayer should be offered in an open place but in case of rain or bad weather or any other reason it can be prayed in a mosque or a hall etc.

**While praying *Janâzah* prayer:**

The *Imâm* should stand level with the head and shoulders of the dead body if the body is male. *Imâm* should stand level with the middle part of the body it is a female.

**Where *Janâzah* prayer differs?**

*Janâzah* prayer is only slightly different from other prayers in that there is no *Rukû'*, no *Sajdah,* and no *Tashhud* in it. There is no fixed time for offering this prayer. It has to be prayed in a standing position only. Other conditions like purification, facing *Qiblah, Sutra,* dress etc. have to be satisfied as in the usual prayers.

**Conduct of *Janâzah* Prayer:**

Like other prayers facing *Qiblah* is a necessary condition. The *Imâm* should ask the people to straighten their rows. There should be an odd number of rows as it is more rewardful.

Making intention is necessary in *Janâzah* prayer as it is necessary in other prayers. Before beginning prayer, the intention should be made in the heart as uttering any words of *Niyat* aloud was not the practice of Prophet Muḥammad (ﷺ) or of his companions.

**First *Takbir* or *Takbir Taḥrimah*:**

*Janâzah* prayer contains 4 *Takbir.* First *Takbir* is *Takbir Taḥrimah.* The *Imam* says *Allâhu Akbar* and raises his hands up to the shoulder level with fingers stretching to the earlobes and the congregation does the same. Then the *Imâm* folds his hands on his chest right hand over the left.

***Du'â* of starting:**

Then the person can read one of those *Du'â* which are recommended in the first *Rak'at* of the usual prayer before recitation of *Fâtiḥah.* For example:

«سُبْحَانَكَ اللَّهُمَّ وَبِحَمْدِكَ وَتَبَارَكَ اسْمُكَ وَتَعَالَى جَدُّكَ وَلَا إِلَهَ غَيْرُكَ»

*"Subḥânaka Allâhumma wa biḥamdika wa tabâra kasmuka wa ta'âla jad-duka walâ ilâha ghayruka."*

"Glory be to You, O Allâh, and all praises are due unto You, and blessed is Your Name and high is Your Majesty and none is worthy of worship but You."

Or he can say other *Du'â*. Some scholars do not recommend *Du'â* of starting in *Janâzah* prayer but reading it is preferable. However, if someone does not read it, it does not affect his prayer. Both ways are practised by Muslim scholars. Then the person should say:

«أَعُوذُ بِاللهِ مِنَ الشَّيْطَانِ الرَّجِيمِ، بِسْمِ اللهِ الرَّحْمَنِ الرَّحِيمِ»

*"A'ûdhu bil-lâhi minash Shaytâ nir-rajeem, Bismillâh hir-Raḥmânir-Raḥeem."*

And then he should recite *Surah Fâtiḥah*.

﴿ٱلْحَمْدُ لِلَّهِ رَبِّ ٱلْعَٰلَمِينَ ﴿٢﴾ ٱلرَّحْمَٰنِ ٱلرَّحِيمِ ﴿٣﴾ مَٰلِكِ يَوْمِ ٱلدِّينِ ﴿٤﴾ إِيَّاكَ نَعْبُدُ وَإِيَّاكَ نَسْتَعِينُ ﴿٥﴾ ٱهْدِنَا ٱلصِّرَٰطَ ٱلْمُسْتَقِيمَ ﴿٦﴾ صِرَٰطَ ٱلَّذِينَ أَنْعَمْتَ عَلَيْهِمْ غَيْرِ ٱلْمَغْضُوبِ عَلَيْهِمْ وَلَا ٱلضَّآلِّينَ﴾ آمين-

*"Alḥamdu lil-lâhi Rab-bil 'âlameen. Ar Raḥmân ir-Raḥeem. Mâliki yawmid-deen. Iyyaka na'budu wa iyyâka nasta'een. Ihdinaṣ ṣirâtal mustaqeem. Ṣirâtal ladheena an'amta 'alayhim. Ghayril maghḍûbi 'alayhim walaḍ ḍâl-leen." Âmeen.*

"Praise in only for Allâh, Lord of the universe. The Most Kind, the Most Merciful. The Master of the Day of Judgment. You Alone we worship and to You Alone we pray for help. Show us the straight way, the way of those whom You have blessed. Who have not deserved Your Anger, nor gone astray."

Some people do not read *Surah Fâtiḥah* in *Janâzah* prayer but *Surah Fâtiḥah* is necessary for the validity of any type of prayer as Prophet Muḥammad (ﷺ) has said that no prayer is valid without *Surah Fâtiḥah*.

Ṭalḥah bin ‘Abdullâh bin ‘Auf (ﷺ) says that he prayed the *Janâzah* prayer behind ‘Abdullâh bin Abbâs (ﷺ) and ‘Abdullâh bin Abbâs (ﷺ) read *Surah Fâtiḥah* aloud. Afterwards he said: “I did read it out loud so that you may know that it is the *Sunnah* of Prophet Muḥammad (ﷺ).” (Bukhâri)

This *Ḥadith* proves that reciting *Surah Fâtiḥah* is necessary in *Janâzah* prayer as well.

**Recitation of a *Surah*:**

A chapter or part of a chapter can be read after the recitiation of *Surah Fâtiḥah* but it is not essential to read it.

**Second *Takbir*:**

Then the *Imâm* should say the second *Takbir* and the congregation should follow but it is not necessary to raise the hands up to the shoulder level but if someone does, it is alright. Both ways are practised by great *‘Ulamâ* and scholars.

**After the second *Takbir*:**

After the second *Takbir,* the person praying *Janâzah* should recite *Darûd* in his heart. It is preferable to read the *Darûd* which a person reads in *Tashahud* of his usual prayer.

**Third *Takbir*:**

Then the *Imâm* should say the third *Takbir* and the congregation should follow. Now, each person should pray for the deceased.

Alternatively the *Imâm* can pray out loud and the congregation can say, *Âmin,* after him. All kinds of *Du‘â* for the benefit of the deceased can be said. Some of these are mentioned below:

***Du‘â* of *Janâzah*:**

1. Abu Hurairah (ﷺ) said that Allâh’s Messenger (ﷺ) prayed *Janâzah* of a Muslim and he said in his *Du‘â* (the following words):

«اللَّهُمَّ اغْفِرْ لِحَيِّنَا وَمَيِّتِنَا وَشَاهِدِنَا وَغَآئِبِنَا وَصَغِيرِنَا وَكَبِيرِنَا وَذَكَرِنَا وَأُنْثَانَا،
اللَّهُمَّ مَنْ أَحْيَيْتَهُ مِنَّا فَأَحْيِهِ عَلَى الْإِسْلَامِ وَمَنْ تَوَفَّيْتَهُ مِنَّا فَتَوَفَّهُ عَلَى
الْإِيمَانِ، اللَّهُمَّ لَا تَحْرِمْنَا أَجْرَهُ وَلَا تُضِلَّنَا بَعْدَهُ» (مسلم)

*"Allâhum maghfirli ḥay-yinâ wa mayyitinâ wa shâhidinâ wa ghâ'ibinâ, wa sagheerina wa kabeeriâ wa dhakarinâ wa unthânâ. Allâhumma man aḥyaytahu min-nâ fa ahyihee 'alal Islâm wa man tawaf-faytahu min-na fatawaf-fahu 'alal imân. Allâhumma lâ taḥrimnâ ajrahu walâ taftin-nâ ba'dahu."* (Muslim, Aḥmad, Abu Dâwûd, Tirmidhi, Ibn Mâjah)

"O Allâh, forgive our people who are still alive and who have passed away, forgive those who are present here and those who are absent, forgive our young and our elderly, forgive our males and females. O Allâh, the one whom You wish to keep alive from among us make him live according to Islam, and anyone whom You wish to die from among us, let him die in belief and faith. O Allâh, do not deprive us from his reward and do not put us is *Fitna* (hardship or any type of trial) after his death."

2. 'Auf bin Mâlik (رضي الله عنه) said that Allâh's Messenger (ﷺ) prayed a *Janâzah* prayer and I heard him saying the following *Du'â* and I memorized it:

«اللَّهُمَّ اغْفِرْ لَهُ وَارْحَمْهُ وَاعْفُ عَنْهُ ة وَعَافِهِ وَأَكْرِمْ نُزُلَهُ وَوَسِّعْ مُدْخَلَهُ
وَاغْسِلْهُ بِالْمَآءِ وَالثَّلْجِ وَالْبَرَدِ وَنَقِّهِ مِنَ الْخَطَايَا كَمَا يُنَقَّي الثَّوْبُ الْأَبْيَضُ
مِنَ الدَّنَسِ وَأَبْدِلْهُ دَارًا خَيْرًا مِّنْ دَارِهِ وَأَهْلًا خَيْرًا مِّنْ أَهْلِهِ وَزَوْجًا خَيْرًا مِّنْ
زَوْجِهِ وَأَدْخِلْهُ الْجَنَّةَ وَقِّهِ فِتْنَةَ الْقَبْرِ وَعَذَابِ النَّارِ»

*"Allâhum maghfirlahu warḥamhu wa'fu 'ânhu wa 'âfihi wa akrim nuzulahu wa was-si' mudkhalahu, waghsilhu bi mâ'i wath thalji wal baradi, wa naq-qihi minal khatâyâ kamâ yunaqqath thawbul abyaḍu minad danasi, wabdilhu dâran khayram min darihi, wa ahlan khayram min ahlihi wa zawjan khayran min zawjihi, wadkhil hul jan-nata, waqihi fitnatal qabri wa 'adha ban nâri."* (Muslim)

"O Allâh, forgive him, have mercy on him, pardon him, grant him security, provide him a nice place and spacious lodgings, wash him with water, snow and ice, purify him from his sins as a white garment is cleansed from dirt, replace his present abode with a better one, replace his present family with a better one, replace his present partner with a better one, make him enter Paradise and save him from the trials of grave and the punishment of Hell."

3. Abu Hurairah (ﷺ) said that Allâh's Messenger (ﷺ) prayed and said:

«اللَّهُمَّ أَنْتَ رَبُّهَا وَأَنْتَ خَلَقْتَهَا وَأَنْتَ رَزَقْتَهَا وَأَنْتَ هَدَيْتَهَا لِلإِسْلَامِ وَأَنْتَ قَبَضْتَ رُوحَهَا وَأَنْتَ أَعْلَمُ بِسِرِّهَا وَعَلَانِيَّتِهَا جِئْنَا شُفَعَاءَ فَاغْفِرْ لَهُ ذَنْبَهُ» (أبو داود وأحمد)

*"Allâhumma anta Rab-buhâ, wa anta khalaqtahâ, wa anta razaqtahâ, wa anta hadaytahâ lil Islâm, wa anta qabaḍta rûḥahâ, wa anta a'lamu bisir-rihâ wa 'alaniyyatihâ, ji'na shufa'â'a, faghfir lahû dhan-bahu."* (Abu Dâwûd and Aḥmad)

"O Allâh, You are its Lord, You have created it, and you have guided it towards Islam, and You have taken out his soul and You know best about its secret and open deeds. We have come as intercessors, so forgive him."

One thing we can see clearly from the above mentioned *Aḥâdith* that every companion who narrated the *Du'â* of *Janâzah* prayer says that he heard the Prophet (ﷺ) saying the words of *Du'â* in *Janâzah* prayer. This proves that Allâh's Messenger (ﷺ) used to say the *Janâzah* prayer or at least the *Du'â* in *Janâzah* prayer aloud. Therefore, there should not be any objection or confusion if the *Imâm* recites aloud in *Janâzah* prayer.

There are some other *Du'â* which are narrated from Prophet Muḥammad (ﷺ) and they can be found in *Ḥadith* books. All of these *Du'â* can be said together or individually. Other *Du'â* can be said with these *Du'â* but it is better to stick to *Du'â* approved by Prophet (ﷺ).

**Ending the *Janâzah* prayer (fourth *Takbir*):**

Then the *Imâm* should say the fourth *Takbir* and the congregation should follow and after that the *Imâm* should say *"As-salâmu 'alaykum wa raḥmatul-lâh*" turning his face to the right first and then to the left; and the congregation should do the same.

**Note:** Some people stress a lot on saying *Du'â* after the completion of *Janâzah* prayer but we did not find a single *Ḥadith* supporting this idea. *Janâzah* prayer is designed so that all the *Du'â* a person wants to say for the deceased can be said after the third *Takbir*. This was the authentic practice of Prophet Muḥammad (ﷺ) and his companions.

## *Ṣalât* (Prayer) during A Journey

Islâm is a practical way of life and considers the situations in which its followers may face difficulties. So Allâh has made the things easy for the believers in such situations. Included in these facilities is the permission for shortening and combining daily prayers during a journey.

***Qaṣr* prayer (short prayer):**

When a Muslim is on a journey he should pray 2 *Rak'at Farḍ* for *Ẓuhr, 'Aṣr* and *'Ishâ*. *Fajr* and *Maghrib* prayers remain as they are.

It is more rewardful to pray a *Qaṣr* prayer (short prayer): It is more rewardful to pray a *Qaṣr* prayer while on a journey. Allâh's Messenger (ﷺ) said:

> *"It is a gift from Allâh which he has bestowed upon you; so you should accept it."* (Muslim)

## Combining *Ṣalât* (Prayer)

A person on a journey can combine *Ẓuhr* and *'Aṣr* prayers together praying them both at *Ẓuhr* or *'Aṣr* time. He can also combine *Maghrib* and *'Ishâ* prayers together praying them both at *Maghrib* or *'Ishâ* time.

Ibn 'Abbâs (رضي الله عنهما) says that Allâh Messenger (ﷺ) used to combine *Ẓuhr* and *'Aṣr* together when he was on a journey and also he used to combine *Maghrib* and *'Ishâ*. (Bukhâri)

Mu'âdh (رضي الله عنه) says that Allâh's Messenger (ﷺ) was on a journey for the battle of Tabook. If the sun had already declined when he wanted to start his journey after having camped somewhere, he would combine his *Ẓuhr* and *'Aṣr* prayers together and pray them both at *Ẓuhr* time, and if he decided to move before the sun had declined then he delayed the *Ẓuhr* prayer and prayed it combined with *'Aṣr* prayer at *'Aṣr* time. And if the sun had already set when he wanted to move he would combine *Maghrib* and *'Ishâ* together at *Maghrib* time. And if the sun had not set when he wanted to move he would delay *Maghrib* and pray it with *'Ishâ* at *'Ishâ* time. (Abu Dâwûd, Tirmidhi)

These *Aḥâdith* are very clear in their meaning an prove that combining prayers while on a journey is a proved and a regular practice of Prophet Muḥammad (ﷺ). Still, there are people who do not believe in combining prayers together while they are travelling. However, this is a gift from Allâh which the believers should accept gratefully and if someone wants to reject Allâh's and His Messenger's offer, it is up to him.

**When to shorten and combine prayers?**

Now, there is the question as to what is the limiting distance and the duration of the journey to make the facility of *Qaṣr* and *Jama'* valid?

a) Yaḥya bin Yazeed said, "I asked Anas bin Mâlik (رضي الله عنه), "When the *Qaṣr* prayer was allowed?" Anas (رضي الله عنه) answered that Allâh's Messenger (ﷺ) whenever he went away about 3 miles he prayed *Qaṣr*." (Muslim, Aḥmad, Abu Dâwûd and Baihaqi)

b) Abu Sa'eed (رضي الله عنه) says that "Whenever *Rasûlûllah* (ﷺ) travelled about 1 *Farsakh* (approximately 3 miles), he would pray *Qaṣr*." (Talkhîs Ibn Ḥajr)

On the basis of these *Aḥâdith,* a person can pray *Qaṣr* and can combine prayers when the distance he travels away from home is 3 miles. This distance is the minimum limit for *Qaṣr* prayer. However, there are many vaired opinions on the minimum limit of the distance for example 9 miles, 48 miles or one days' journey etc.

In our opinion the correct definition of a journey is what the society as a whole recognizes unde their circumstances, the minimum limit being 3 miles.

**Duration of journey:**

A person can prays *Qaṣr* and combine his prayers for as long as he remains on a journey, whether it takes weeks, months or years. Even if he stays put in one place to fulfil the purpose of his journey he can continue to pray *Qaṣr* and combine his prayers. However, if he intended to stay in a place for a fixed number of days then the opinions differ on how long he can go on combining and shortening his prayers, e.g. 4 days, 10 days, 17 days, 18 days etc.

After a careful study of *Aḥâdith*, we can say that when someone stays in a fixed place temporarily he would be considered a traveller on a journey, and there is no limit on the number of days he can pray *Qaṣr* and combine his prayers.

***Nafl* prayer on a journey:**

Prophet (ﷺ) always offered *Witr* prayer during his journey and he emphasized and expressed the importance of 2 *Rak'at Sunnat* of the *Fajr* prayer. Therefore, the believers should pray these, while on a journey. But what about any other *Nafl* and *Sunnat* prayer? The following *Ḥadith* answers this question:

Ḥafs bin 'Aṣim says, "I accompanied 'Abdullâh bin 'Umar (رضي الله عنهما) on a journey to Makkah. On the way to Makkah he led us in the *Ẓuhr* prayer and offered 2 *Rak'at*. Then he went to sit in his tent. He saw some people praying and asked me what they were doing. "They are praying *Nafl*", said I. Then he said, "If I could pray *Nafl* then I should have prayed the complete *Farḍ* prayer." Then he continued, "I accompanied Allâh's Messenger on a journey. He did not pray during his travels more than 2 *Rak'at*. Then I accompanied Abu Bakr, 'Umar and 'Uthmân and they did the same as Prophet Muḥammad (ﷺ). There is a good example for you in the practice of Prophet Muḥammad (ﷺ)." (Bukhâri)

There are some other *Aḥâdith* which prove that some of the companions used to pray *Nafl* during their journey. It is better not to pray *Nafl* while travelling, but if you stay somewhere and have time you may do so.